TRACING THE HISTORY OF
YOUR HOUSE

TRACING THE HISTORY OF
YOUR HOUSE

PETER BUSHELL

PAVILION
MICHAEL JOSEPH

First published in Great Britain in 1989 by
PAVILION BOOKS LIMITED
196 Shaftesbury Avenue, London WC2H 8JL
in association with Michael Joseph Limited
27 Wrights Lane, Kensington, London W8 5TZ

Designed by Janet James

A CIP catalogue record for this book is
available from the British Library

ISBN 1-85145-315-6

Printed and bound in Great Britain
by Butler and Tanner Ltd
Frome and London

This book is dedicated to
ANNE C. COZENS
She knows why . . . and so do I

Contents

Prologue

Several years ago, and like many struggling young writers, I had a consuming ambition to see myself in print. To this end I decided to write a book on the more bizarre (and less well-known) aspects of London. During the five years I spent researching and writing this I read more than seven hundred books on the capital, severely damaging my eyesight.

The completed work ran to more than twelve hundred pages of manuscript disposed through four volumes. Its value – at least in my own mind – was that it was less a guide book than a fascinating ramble through English social history, using London landmarks as hooks on which to hang stories about the people who had populated it down the centuries. (People have always been my primary interest. Without them a house is merely a haphazard collection of bricks devoid of personality and meaning.)

I sent this vast tome to Constable and Co. The word came back: 'Cut it and we'll publish'. This I did. The work ultimately appeared in 1983 under the title: *London's Secret History*. At the time of writing it has sold more than ten thousand copies.

While I was naturally pleased by this success it left me with a residual regret. My original twelve hundred pages had been reduced in published form to less than two hundred and fifty. I had to face the fact that in practical terms this meant almost 75 per cent of the time I had invested in the project had been wasted.

Nevertheless – and because I had no inclination to produce *London's Secret History II* – it looked as if there was no way round the impasse. Then, about a year after publication, as I was idly leafing through this material one wet Monday and mourning its uselessness, it occurred to me that there *might* be a market for it after all. Why not dispose of it piecemeal – to individuals and business concerns occupying premises or sites about which I had acquired interesting information?

I began by sending letters to a hundred prospective business clients, offering to have the information I had gleaned printed up and framed. In this way it could be hung in their boardroom as an object of general interest or in the reception area as a focus for visiting executives.

To the best of my knowledge the project was unique. I therefore had no idea of the reaction I might expect. Some of my friends, with experience of mail-shot canvassing, indicated I'd receive a positive response of between one and two per cent. In the event, one in ten clients expressed an interest – thus enabling me to climb down the academic ladder and begin selling history in the market-place as a 'house detective'.

Since then I have written the histories of more than a thousand sites and dwellings covering almost every kind of structure from Mayfair mansions to country manor houses, bijou suburban villas, artisans' terraced cottages, modern office blocks, a water-pumping station and – for a highly respectable and deeply conservative bank – a circus site (where I discovered Billy Smart's ancient Rolls Royce rusting forgotten beneath an old tarpaulin).

The wide-ranging nature of these commissions shows that it is quite wrong to assume that only older properties are interesting or distinguished. Almost every structure which has been in existence for fifty years or more is in some way special and has its own unique story to relate. A 1920s house proved to have an association with Dylan Thomas; an Edwardian villa had once been the home of a notorious female confidence trickster; a house of a similar period was found to have belonged to the music hall star, Jessie Matthews; while Mavis Wheeler (the wife of the archaeologist, Sir Mortimer Wheeler), who in the 1950s served a term of imprisonment for putting three bullets into her lover, Lord Vivian, once lived in a very unprepossessing 1950s flat in Salisbury.

The White House – which forms the subject of Chapter Eight of this book – is a perfect example of how a relatively modern property can prove to be of surprising interest.

The house is occupied today by the Managing Director of Pavilion Books, Colin Webb. In the spring of 1987 Colin approached me with the idea for this book after seeing an article on my work in a London evening newspaper. He suggested that we might use the White House as one of three case histories (now reproduced as Part Three).

I was initially disinclined to accept the offer. I wasn't sure the time was right for me to write another book; and I knew nothing about the White House or its history. However, I was driven to accept by an intrinsic love of a challenge – and my firm belief that every house has a story to tell.

History, however, does not always play its cards face up. (It frequently failed to do so in the case of the White House.) Consequently, like every other aspect of detective work, tracing the history of a building may require patience. In order to come to some estimate of when your house was constructed it is essential to read Part One of this book with care.

Thereafter it may be necessary to spend several days sifting through archival material in search of significant facts. This is often tedious work. I can only say that the feeling one experiences when a significant fact is finally persuaded to give itself up is like no other I have ever experienced. It provides a sense of elation, a kind of 'high', which is curiously addictive. (Anyone doubting this should look in at the Central Registry of Births, Deaths and Marriages on any given day and observe the crush of people tracing their ancestors.)

But if nothing worthwhile comes easily, and if the task is sometimes difficult, it is almost never impossible. The rewards are incalculable. In the end it only requires the expertise to uncover the facts and the wit to interpret them . . . honestly and without embellishment.

This book is a step-by-step guide for the amateur house-historian who wishes to have the pleasure and deep satisfaction of doing so for himself.

Peter Bushell.
London. 1988

PART ONE

THE
FABRIC

Dating the Exterior

I t is commonly believed that the most effective method for dating a house is to start with the earliest known 'fact' and work forward to the present day.

While superficially logical, the weakness in this approach is that if 'fact' proves to be rumour and rumour plays us false, then the process founders before it has begun.

If the 'fact' at first holds up, but is later discredited, there is a strong possibility that everything based upon it will prove equally false . . . causing the whole premise to come tumbling about our heads like a pack of cards.

To start at the beginning is as sensible as a policeman setting a murder investigation in train by calling for reports of the victim's birth. In fact, like all good detectives, we start with what we know – and work backwards.

The first step involves a visit to the scene of the crime – in this case a close external inspection of the house, looking at it with fresh eyes. When doing so, it is important to bear in mind that the modern habit of pigeon-holing architectural styles – 'Elizabethan', 'Queen Anne', 'Georgian' – can be extremely misleading.

Fashions in architecture do not cease at the precise moment that the monarchs who have given them their name breathe their last. Consequently there are many fine examples of buildings 'Georgian' in spirit but not in fact because they were erected well into the reign of Queen Victoria. Similarly there are several London structures of solidly 'Edwardian' design put up as late as 1919 – the eighth year of the reign of Edward VII's son, George V.

The first task in dating a building is to determine its general shape. Until the end of the seventeenth century many small dwellings had only one room per floor, which ran from front to back. The existence of more than one suggests that some form of interior reconstruction has taken place.

Similarly, it is important to pay as much attention to the rear of the property as the front. Occupants often updated the showy aspect of a dwelling in a very literal attempt to keep up appearances. They were seldom as zealous when it came to those sections not immediately exposed to view, such as the rear and the servants' quarters.

A careful inspection should quickly determine whether the building is essentially symmetrical – in which case it is unlikely to be earlier than the late seventeenth century. If the positioning of the chimney-stacks, the windows and the doors are in proportion to the rest of the house, and their general style is also compatible, there is every chance that it remains more or less as built.

If, however, they strike the eye as being irregular, or if windows or doors give the appearance of being of a later date, they may well be additions imposed on an earlier structure. However, unless the house has been substantially rebuilt, they almost certainly occupy their original position. It is one thing to re-render a wall. It is quite another to re-site doors, windows and chimney-stacks. Apart from the expense involved, there would have been little reason.

In the case of a large building, where there are genuine grounds for believing that a house has been radically altered or even rebuilt on the site of an earlier dwelling, an aerial photograph can be of enormous benefit in reconstructing the previous layout. It is, however, very expensive.

★   ★   ★

Until the canals and then the railways provided means of transporting heavy goods all over the country, most building materials came from the immediate surrounding area. The most common of these was timber.

There are few surviving timber-framed buildings constructed much before 1500. Those that do survive are for the most part well documented. They were originally in-filled with wattle and daub. This was sometimes later replaced by plaster or a mixture of plaster and weather-boarding. Where a timber-framed house is not typical of an area, or where the framing appears inconsistent with the rest of the dwelling, it should be regarded with suspicion. Timber-framed houses of the Tudor period were mostly occupied by the upper middle class – gentry and merchants. Because the timber was frequently re-used – thus explaining the meaningless mortice holes which are sometimes apparent in non-structural timbers today – it is extremely difficult to date such buildings.

A second early building constituent was cob, which had the appearance of concrete and was fashioned from straw, mud and chalk. Cob was mainly used in dwellings constructed for the lower classes.

Woven lath (oak)

Cob houses can often be identified by the tapered aspect of the external walls which are usually much thicker at the base than the top. By the nineteenth century many cob houses had been re-faced with brick.

Logically enough, houses constructed of stone were usually sited within two days' journey of a quarry. This is especially evident in such areas as the Cotswolds, where every other dwelling appears to be fashioned from the local honey-coloured oolitic limestone.

As only the rich could afford to use great rectangular-cut (ashlar) blocks, the poor had to make do with houses fashioned from rubble, irregular (but nonetheless sizeable) off-cuts. These humble dwellings were usually lime-washed to protect them against the elements.

As fashions changed, tenants commonly sought to remove the limewash and expose the bare stone. Fortunately for the historian, limewash is notoriously difficult to remove and almost impossible to remove without trace. Any wall retaining flakes of limewash almost certainly dates from at least the nineteenth century.

Although their number has diminished in the last hundred years, there are still a few houses dotted around the country constructed from Coade stone. Manufactured through an artificial process by Eleanor Coade of Lambeth, examples of it survive in London in the form of the South Bank Lion, the urns which decorate the parapet of the southern facade of Somerset House, and the tomb of Captain Bligh (of the *Bounty*) in the churchyard of St Mary's, Lambeth. Houses of Coade stone were always rare and there will never be any more. The manufacturing process has been lost.

When examining any stone-built house with a view to determining its date and authenticity there are certain basic questions which must always be asked: how easy would it have been to transport the stone to the site in the days when transport was difficult; how does the manner in which it has been laid conform to that of other houses in the area; and could the material have been salvaged from a previous house, either on this site or elsewhere?

Timber-framed houses

Sixteenth-century
thatched cottage

The last but most common building material to consider is brick. Imported into England by the Romans, it ceased to be used after their departure and remained out of favour until the Middle Ages.

By about 1560 the more well-off were constructing their chimneys from brick; and by about 1688 – the year the deposed James II was cowering against the windswept church tower of St Mary's, Lambeth, waiting for a boat to carry him into exile – brick was in very common use. It is possible to date brick-built houses of this period fairly accurately because bricks were then both longer and slimmer than now.

In 1784 the Brick Tax was introduced. As this was levied on the number of bricks used rather than the area covered, bricks suddenly became very large, the average size being $10'' \times 5'' \times 3''$.

In 1803 further legislation had the effect of reducing the normal size to $9'' \times 4\frac{1}{2}'' \times 3''$. By the mid-Victorian era most bricks were machine-produced to a standard size. With some exceptions, mostly in the north of England, Victorian brickwork averaged four courses (or layers) to the foot.

An additional aid in determining the age of a brick-built house is the 'bond', or pattern of brick-laying, employed. (See diagrams overleaf.) The earliest bricklayers used no regular bond. English Bond, which consists of alternate courses of headers (laid end on) and stretchers (laid lengthways on) was widely used until the end of the seventeenth century. So was Garden Wall Bond – two courses of stretchers followed by a course of headers.

At the end of the seventeenth century Flemish Bond, which is composed of courses which alternate headers and stretchers, came into fashion and attained widespread popularity. In some cases the headers employed in

A

B

C

A Stretcher
B Header
C Flemish Bond
D English Garden Wall Bond
E English Bond
F Flemish Stretcher Bond
G Header Bond
H Stretcher Bond

D

E

F

G

H

Flemish Bond were burned to a darker finish, thus providing an unusual decorative effect.

The maverick among bonds – Stretcher Bond – consists entirely of bricks laid lengthways. It is commonly used for walls only 4½″ thick and is a fair indication of modern cavity walling.

After examining the bonding, we should next look at the exterior brickwork for signs of additions – both outwards and upwards. Variations in pattern or brick-colour at the top of a house indicate the roof may have been raised at some point, possibly to provide the topmost rooms with a greater ceiling height, or even repair work due to bomb damage.

Having taken all the above points into account we should now have a reasonable understanding of the basic shell of our building. We must next examine the detail – starting with the doors, the windows and the roof.

Tudor doors, which were often arch-shaped, were lower than those of today because people were much shorter. Doors were hung either directly on to the walls or from a heavy but rudimentary timber frame.

Square-framed doors began to make an appearance about the middle of the seventeenth century. Front doors were mainly of oak and sometimes protected from the elements by a porch. By the end of the eighteenth century many of these old-style porches had been superseded by the less functional but more decorative open variety.

Detail of iron handle
on studded door

Door with porch

Windows too had become more decorative, a far cry from those of the early fifteenth century when glass was available only to the very rich. In the reign of Richard III – and afterwards Henry VII – these were often no more than long and low timber-framed holes divided into lights by stone uprights and protected by interior wooden shutters. This remained the fashion until the influence of the mid seventeenth century Renaissance movement caused them to elongate.

The mullioned window was also then very popular – and remained so until replaced by the Georgian sash, fashioned from timber. Initially, sash windows were installed flush to the exterior brickwork. In 1707 a Building Act was passed requiring that for the future they should be rebated 4″.

Although there is a tendency to assume that all 'blocked' windows are a relic of the Window Tax which was introduced in 1695 and remained in force for most of the eighteenth century, this is not always the case. There are several exceptions. Blocked windows are sometimes evidence of interior reconstruction which rendered them obsolete. There is also the possibility that they were constructed in this manner on purpose. The Georgians developed an obsession for perfectly proportioned buildings and often inserted 'blind' windows in order to retain the overall symmetry. In some instances they even went so far as to have them painted to resemble their more functional counterparts. (I know of at least one house where a blocked window has been painted in the 'open' position in order to show something of the 'interior'.)

When endeavouring to determine the authenticity of a window it is important to examine the head, jambs and sill. In some instances wall disturbance will indicate signs of 'restoration'.

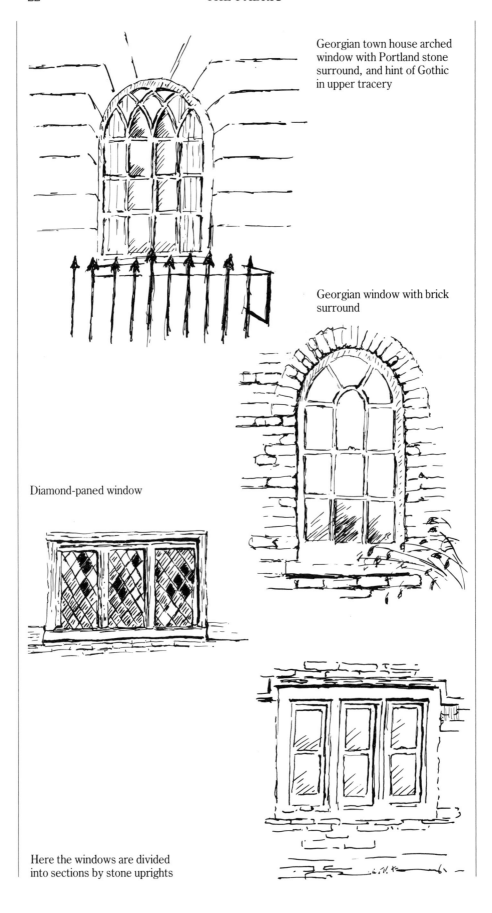

Georgian town house arched
window with Portland stone
surround, and hint of Gothic
in upper tracery

Georgian window with brick
surround

Diamond-paned window

Here the windows are divided
into sections by stone uprights

In the case of seventeenth-century mullioned windows fitted with leaded lights, firm authentication can be extremely difficult. Many old mullioned windows have been salvaged from original sites and installed in alien structures. There is no infallible way of spotting this. One can only look for discrepancies in style with other features of the house. It is, however, useful to remember that when dealing with out-and-out fakes, the original leaded panes were coarse of finish, often tinted yellow or green, and rectangular in shape. Victorian reproductions use a smoother form of glass and the panes tend to be diamond-shaped. 'Bull's eyes' glass – which was very inferior and only used in the cheapest form of housing – is nearly always fake or alien. It nonetheless often makes inappropriate appearances in an attempt to lend dwellings a spurious 'period' character.

(e)

(f)

Bull's eye glass

Victorian rectangular door
with Ham stone surround

As walls, doors and windows tend to be relatively durable they are less difficult to date than roof-coverings, which in the course of several centuries may have been replaced several times. Tiles and slate have an average life expectancy of a hundred years. If properly laid, thatch lasts about sixty years.

In this respect original roofs can have a lot in common with the headsman's axe which – said Stanley Holloway in one of his famous monologues – 'as 'ad a new 'andle and p'raps a new 'ead, but it's a real old original axe'.

By and large, the steeper the pitch of a roof the older its foundation. In centuries gone by both materials and construction techniques were wanting. Consequently, roofs had to be built on a steeper gradient to repel rain and snow more quickly – before it had the chance to penetrate.

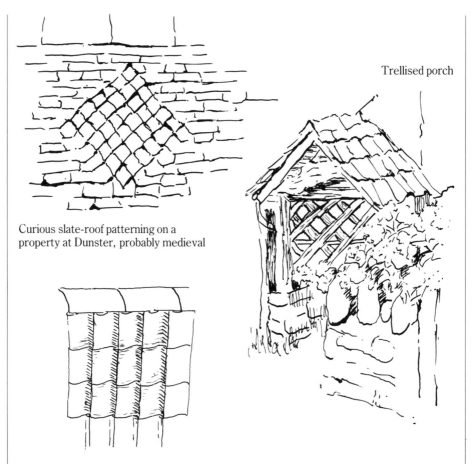

Trellised porch

Curious slate-roof patterning on a
property at Dunster, probably medieval

Section of pantile roofing

Until about 1460 nearly every small house was either thatched or shingled –
thin slabs of oak fixed with wooden pegs. Tiles began to achieve prominence
around 1500, although they were more irregular in shape than now. Where
they replaced thatch, evidence sometimes survives of a redundant 'weather-
ing' course of stone or brick which is visible above the present roof line.

The pantile – a decorative form of tile, Flemish in conception – began to
make an impression in the east and west of England in the seventeenth
century. Curiously, it was used in the West Country less for houses than for
farm buildings.

By this date slate was also widely used as a roof covering although – until
the Industrial Revolution – most commonly in the areas of source: Cornwall,
the Lake District and Wales. Cheap and durable, it attained considerable
popularity with the working and artisan classes. This in time brought it into
disrepute and it became indelibly associated with the slum terraces of the
North and the Valleys. In the late Victorian era the occupants of slate-roofed
dwellings in less deprived areas sought to distance themselves from this
image of poverty and deprivation by re-roofing in tile. Consequently, many
slate quarries fell into disuse.

Before turning to the clues harboured by the interior of a building, we should
spare a moment to examine three more external factors: the chimney-stacks,

Early 19th-century
chimney-stack with pots

Victorian chimney-
stack with 'crown' pots

Late 19th-century
downpipe

the gutters and downpipes; and – where applicable – any fire insurance
badges.

Chimney-stacks tell us a good deal about the layout of a house. In their
present form they first came into regular use in the mid-sixteenth century,
when they were made from stone or brick or sometimes both. By the
eighteenth century many of them were elaborately decorated.

By comparison very ugly, the Victorian chimney-pot was devised to help
improve the drawing qualities of the coal fire. Coal was then replacing wood as
the country's primary fuel source.

Until cast iron was introduced in the nineteenth century, gutters and
downpipes were mostly fashioned from lead, sometimes with an outer casing
of wood.

Some of these downpipes actually bear a date. Although it can be sorely
tempting to believe that the date of the downpipe is the date of the house, this
is not always the case. For instance, a dwelling with a slate, but formerly
thatched, roof will almost certainly predate its gutterings – because thatched
roofs were seldom fitted with them.

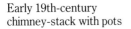

Fire badges, examples above, are a relic of the days when insurance
companies maintained their own private fire-fighting forces. Most incorporate
a number. It was sometimes customary for the badge to be replaced on an
annual basis following payment of the premium, in which case the year for
which it was valid was also inscribed. The existence of such a date is therefore
not a reliable guide to the age of the house.

It was as well to belong to one of these fire-fighting 'clubs'. Failure to do so could mean ruination. Nonetheless, membership provided no absolute guarantee of immunity. The members of one fire brigade, which kept its equipment in the churchyard of St James's, in London's Piccadilly, found themselves so exhausted after pushing their water-cart the short distance to Albemarle Street that they were able neither to work the pump nor climb the ladder. In consequence the house burned down.

On a brighter note, many of these early insurance companies kept extremely accurate records of house contents. In some cases these records survive – either in the archives of the insurance company or those of its successors. As they enable us to 'refurnish' the interior of the property room by room, very often down to the ormolu clock on the drawing-room mantelpiece and the colour of the carpet on the floor, they represent a priceless historical tool. Sometimes there are plans attached, which can provide a guide to subsequent structural alterations to the fabric. These are, frankly, very rare. Where they survive they can provide invaluable information on the way in which rooms were originally disposed. As a client of mine, David Wood, commented:

> We have discovered that our basement was originally built as a billiard room. This explains the mystery of a strange narrow sentry-box-like feature indented in one wall. It was obviously a place to keep the billiard cues. Information gleaned from original plans can be fascinating. For instance, the room my wife uses for sewing was originally the Morning Room, but by 1929 had been changed into the Servants' Hall. This room overlooks the garden and it would have been unthinkable, thirty years earlier, for the servants to look out upon their masters at recreation!

He continues:

> Similarly, my office was originally the Drawing Room, and the main Lounge or Sitting Room was the Dining Room. This explained to us the strange layout . . . and the position of the fireplace – around which it has always been impossible to place sofas successfully without blocking access to the Hall. Yet one can see a dining room table fitting in the room perfectly.

Journey into the Interior

Many of the features which helped us to an understanding of the exterior of the building – the roof, the chimneys, the doors, windows and walls – will be of equal benefit when studying the interior. On the basis that the space beneath it may well be the least altered part of the building we should begin with the roof.

As explained in the previous chapter, roofs themselves are not especially durable. Precisely because of this they have almost certainly left a number of clues, most of which tell a story.

Where structural beams form part of the original main frame – which can often be determined by comparing their disposition to the chimney-stacks – they are especially useful in helping to date a property.

Many of the trusses, secured to the tie or collar beam, would have been fashioned elsewhere and delivered to the site for assembly. In order to ensure that they were assembled correctly, many would have been numbered.

Where this numbering survives it represents a useful aide to pinpointing alterations: you can determine whether numbered beams have been removed and whether they have been replaced or supplemented by those which are not numbered.

A study of all the beams in the house will also show whether they date from the sixteenth century (or before) – when it was the practice to chamfer (or splay) the outer angles of a beam quite deeply; or some time after that, when the chamfering became more shallow.

The fact that chamfering tended to terminate or 'stop' a little before meeting the wall is another useful guide to dating. Generally speaking, the less elaborate the 'stop' the older the beam. Charred or blackened roof beams indicate that the house may once have possessed an open hall – an additional indication that any upper floor was almost certainly an afterthought.

It is a truth generally acknowledged – and often repeated – that you get what you pay for. It is as true of beams as of anything else. The beams of humble cottages tended to be rough-hewn and poorly finished. In the houses of the rich they were bigger, better and frequently moulded with classical or Gothic designs.

In the eighteenth century, when ornamental plaster ceilings came into vogue, many beams disappeared from view, encased in boarding or plaster, where they were left to slumber until returned to life by the hand of the twentieth-century 'restorer', not always to a room's benefit.

All beams should be examined for dowel and mortice holes, grooves and slots which appear to serve no purpose. They may once have been load-bearing beams or beams forming part of a partition, since removed. They may occupy their original site, or have been brought here from some other part of the house – or some other site entirely. There is even a chance that they are old ships' timbers – a remote but romantic possibility deeply cherished by most beam-owning householders, especially those living furthest from the sea. Beams inserted purely for decoration are seldom jointed to the main load-bearing timbers.

Having thoroughly explored the beams we should now turn to the walls. These should be examined in detail, preferably with the palm of the hand, for any tell-tale cracks or crevices. Recesses in-filled with rubble or plaster may once have held cupboards. What are now cupboards may possibly have been constructed within spaces formerly occupied by windows. The thickness of the walls is also a factor. As the centuries passed, building techniques produced walls of increasing thinness.

In ancient times, walls were coated with a primitive form of plaster made from lime and sand. This provided the thinnest of coverings and the process would have needed to be repeated several times in order to be effective. Seventeenth-century builders employed a thicker plaster, sometimes rein-forced with animal hair, which acted as a binder. The Victorians utilised Portland cement which, being a great deal more pure than any of its forerunners, allowed a smoother finish.

Most walls in a house of any antiquity will retain traces of several forms of plasterwork. The same may well hold true for the wallpaper. Wallpaper first came into common use in the nineteenth century. Where it is possible to recover fragments of genuinely old wallpaper or plaster these should be taken to the local museum where officials may be able to help in fixing their date.

In exceptional cases, a careful examination of an interior wall will reveal a window, completely intact, plastered over centuries before.

Similarly, care in investigating present windows may reveal evidence of enlargement, enclosure or foreshortening. As many windows were previously fitted with shutters, traces of the fittings may yet survive in the form of redundant staples or in-filled screw holes which formerly supported the securing iron bar.

In the case of sash windows it is sometimes possible to locate small square patches of discoloured woodwork in the running frame, the site of wooden blocks, since removed, used to restrict the degree to which the window could be opened.

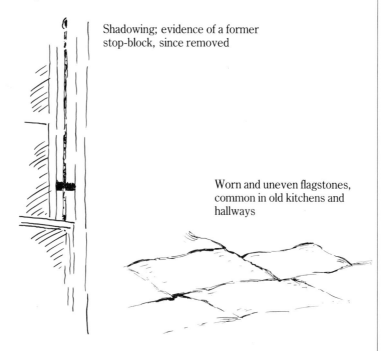

Shadowing; evidence of a former stop-block, since removed

Worn and uneven flagstones, common in old kitchens and hallways

Medieval floors were composed of compressed earth covered with rushes. These were replaced by rough-hewn flagstones, in turn replaced in the seventeenth century by floors of brick and tile. The tiles were usually unglazed and significantly larger than the tiles of today.

Timber floors are a relatively modern innovation. Builders were working almost exclusively in oak until about 1680; but generally speaking most houses did not have timber floors until the eighteenth century, and then only in the principal domestic rooms. The old hardwood floorboards were invariably dowelled and rather larger than their modern deal counterparts. A clear discrepancy in floor levels – and the materials used to fashion them – is evidence that the area may once have boasted an open hall.

The kitchen and the servants' quarters may well have remained flagged well into the present century. In some cases the kitchen floor was constructed at a lower level than the other floors in the house to facilitate drainage.

Sadly, although they often constitute an owner's pride and joy, doors have a nasty habit of proving cuckoos. Easily portable, they were frequently moved from one room to another or brought from another house.

Timber has always been plentiful. This made it possible, as styles changed, for doors simply to be replaced with something more fashionable. Where this has occurred it may be possible to spot the deception by removing the architrave – the moulding which covers the joint between the door and the wall – which can reveal an original and probably much heavier frame beneath. Fake doors tend to be less solid than the originals, which were usually not hinged but hung on iron pins and rides. As a general rule, old doors are rather square in shape, fakes and modern ones more rectangular.

Georgian architrave

As we have seen, unexplained grooves or holes in beams are evidence of a former use, possibly as supports for some long-gone partition. Most early partitions were fashioned from timber and in-filled with wattle and daub. As time progressed, this in-filling was replaced by grooved oak planks, joined one to the next and secured at top and bottom by slotting into the timber frame.

Like the doors, these timber partitions suffered heavily at the hands of fashion. Some were removed, others painted or even plastered over. A similar fate often befell a house's panelling.

Although many people tend to associate panelling with the Tudor era in England, it was popular in the better class of household some time before that. Its original purpose was functional rather than decorative: to reduce heat-loss and combat draughts. Most early panelling was fashioned from local hardwoods. In the course of time, and in the cases of those who could afford it, the panels grew larger and more decorative.

Despite its obvious beauty, by the seventeenth century oak panelling had become unfashionable. It was replaced by pine, which was often painted over. Pine was itself superseded as a popular wall-covering towards the end of the eighteenth century by ornamental plasterwork and wallpaper.

When making an interior examination of the fireplaces in a house it is important to remember that all is not necessarily what it seems. There may be more – or less.

It is quite possible that the relatively modest fireplace of today conceals a much larger one, closed in during the mid-eighteenth century by some

Georgian householder at a time when coal was beginning to replace half tree-trunks as the primary source of heating.

Inversely, some grand 'Tudor' hearth may prove to be a fake. If so, it can probably be established fairly easily. A builder seeking to recreate the glories of the Elizabethan era might be prepared to insert an impressive and

17th-century fireplace of Ham stone

authentic-looking fireplace. He would almost certainly not have been prepared to sacrifice precious living accommodation by inserting a vast Elizabethan flue.

Many genuine Tudor fireplaces incorporated a bread-oven. Some would also have had a circular or semicircular area recessed within one of the fireplace's interior side-walls. Many householders believe these to have been priests' holes. In fact, they were probably never used for anything less pedestrian than the curing of bacon.

To the best of my knowledge – and with one curious exception – all houses possess a staircase. The exception was Apsley House, at Hyde Park Corner, afterwards the home of the great Duke of Wellington. Lord Apsley insisted on designing his new town-house himself. A great gourmet (and a greater glutton) it was close to completion before he realized that he had forgotten to make provision for getting from his dining-room to his bed.

The first form of staircase was little more than a primitive ladder. This was replaced by an all-purpose central staircase, usually spiral in design and fashioned from wood or stone. It was situated close by the hearth or set into the gable wall. An example of the latter survives at the ruined Minster Lovell Hall in Oxfordshire.

From the sixteenth century four main types of staircase predominated: the semi-circular newel stairway; the straight-flight variety which ascends between two walls; the dog-leg stair which turns back on the previous flight by means of a landing; and the open-well stair – a grander version of the dog-leg – most commonly seen in large town-houses and country mansions.

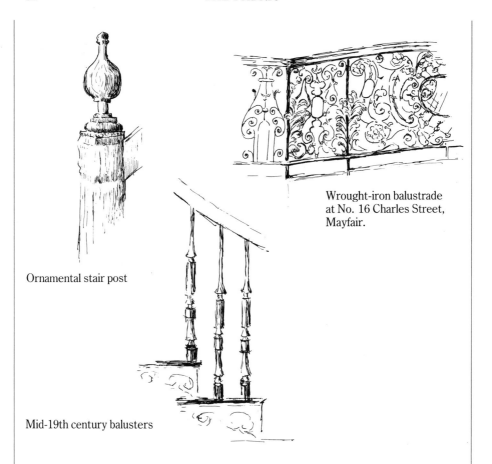

Ornamental stair post

Wrought-iron balustrade
at No. 16 Charles Street,
Mayfair.

Mid-19th century balusters

It was these grander houses which first introduced the concept of the baluster, in other words the open-sided staircase, which began to make its appearance in the sixteenth century. As time progressed, balusters reduced in thickness and increased in elegance.

As we have seen, in an era when labour was cheap but building materials expensive, it was not uncommon for portable features to be removed from one house to another. Panelling, doors, Georgian fireplaces, were all treated in this way. Ceiling joists and beams became a common target for the 'restorer'. New beams, with their smooth machine-cut edge were adzed to produce an artificial 'hand-cut' effect. Other machines mass-produced 'Georgian' cornices and decorative pieces of plasterwork by the thousand. (They are distinguishable by their unnatural symmetry and the fact that they tend to look stuck on.)

As a result, it is extremely dangerous to attempt to date a property on the evidence of such features alone. They have to be considered in relation to other, circumstantial, evidence; and as any detective will confirm, circumstantial evidence, while not especially dramatic, is nearly always the most reliable. Conversely, there is no more certain recipe for disaster than endeavouring to force the fat square peg of an opinion into the lean round hole of a fact.

The situation is aggravated by the large number of hybrid dwellings almost entirely constructed in this dubious manner. The most cunning is Bailiffscourt (opposite page), a 'medieval manor house' at Climping in West

Sussex. It is now a superb hotel. I quote from the brochure:

> This unique set of buildings was brought together in the 1930s by
> the late Lord Moyne; a replica of Sir Roger de Montgomery's
> 13th-century courthouse originally tended by bailiff monks.   ˙
>
> Each stone, window and doorway comes from that period, all
> long and earnestly sought after throughout Southern England.
> Pieces from derelict mansions, farmhouses and cottages were
> brought back to Climping, to be lovingly and expertly refashioned
> into this rambling masterpiece . . .

Enthusiastic antiquarians such as Lord Moyne represent the house
historian's perfect nightmare. They are carriers of the Real Old Original Axe
Syndrome in its most virulent form.

It would be quite wrong, however, to infer from all this that no house can
ever be dated or authenticated. With patience and understanding, by
comparing the property under review with houses of a similar period and
design, it is nearly always possible to do so, at the very least approximately.

That said . . . our preliminary survey is at an end. We are now almost
ready to seek the advice of the professionals. Before we do so it may be useful
to draw up a plan of the house. Although it is obviously best to include as much
detail as possible, in some cases a sketch of the basic dimensions will do.

Drawing Up a House Plan

To draw up a house plan you will require the following items:

A wooden expanding ruler
A steel tape
A clip-board
A rubber
A sharp pencil
A pad of plain or squared paper
A drawing-board
A T-square
A set-square
A compass
A compass extension piece (for large dimensions)
Spring bows (for small dimensions)

1 The first task should be to take photographs of all the exterior elevations. These should be square-on. Angled photographs distort perspective and are' therefore of very little use.

2 Photographs – or drawings, if you prefer – should be made of any interesting external or internal feature. Additionally, each room should be photographed from at least two different perspectives.

3 The photography completed, we can make a start on the internal plan. For large buildings the best scale to use is one of eight feet to the inch. For smaller buildings it can be four feet to the inch.

4 Metric measurements may be substituted if desired, but it is as well to remember that you may later wish to compare your findings with those in any ancient plans you come across. The measurements in these will almost certainly have been made in feet and inches.

5 Because the plan needs to be reasonably accurate, measuring should not be undertaken single-handed. The ideal number of collaborators is three: one to measure, one to steady the tape or ruler and one to annotate.

6 Each room on a floor should be measured before proceeding to the next storey.

7 Working clockwise, take the measurement of each wall, including, where possible, its thickness. 'Breaks' in the wall – such as windows, doorways, recesses or built-up openings – should be measured as encountered.

8 In addition to taking the dimensions of the door itself, remember to calculate:

  a the door-swing, and
  b the measurements of the door 'space'
  – i.e. the void left by the door
  when open, not including the jamb

9 Having completed the measurement of all the above, measure the height to the ceiling.

10 Next, take a diagonal measurement of the room at floor level. One diagonal measurement will do, but two is better, because in this way we build up a series of triangles which help to show whether or not the room is square. Many old buildings are very far from being so.

11 Before proceeding to the next room, note any apparent changes in floor level.

12 Having taken the measurement of all the rooms, proceed to the roof in order to measure and calculate the disposition of the timbers or other form of construction.

13 It will also be necessary to measure the angle of roof-pitch. If, for some reason, it is not possible to gain access to the roof space, the angle of pitch can probably be calculated externally by taking the measurement of the external ridge at the end gable wall.

14 Finally, calculate the overall external measurements of the house. In doing so, chimney-stacks should be discounted. Where a house is built of brick, height can be calculated by counting the number of courses. In relatively modern houses, the courses rise four to the foot. In older dwellings the bricks vary from modern standards. Consequently it will be necessary to measure a sample area and calculate accordingly.

15 When all these procedures have been carried out the information should be incorporated into a drawn plan, one for each room or section of the building. In compiling these plans it is advisable to use tracing paper so that it will be possible at a later stage to superimpose them over details of any earlier plans which may be lodged in local archives. As a precaution against loss, it is best to make at least one additional copy of the finished plans.

Window with leaded lights

Pandora's Box

County Records Offices

County Records Offices are the primary source of information for anyone wishing to know more about the history of their houses. They are normally – although not always – situated in the county town. In some instances they have premises of their own, in others they are housed as a separate entity within the principal local library.

Conditions vary considerably and usually reflect the degree of importance given to local history by the ruling Authority. For instance, the Oxfordshire County Records Office is located in a cramped basement of a municipal office block. Consequently, the number of seats is severely restricted. They nearly always have to be booked in advance. In contrast, the County Records Office at Exeter occupies spacious, airy premises with ample seating for everyone.

Because of these variations in conditions and procedure, it is always wise to make a preliminary telephone call before making a visit. Some Records Offices do retain a number of seats for 'chance' callers, but the practice is far from widespread.

Many of them have limited opening hours, and most close for lunch. Those that remain open operate a restricted service during this period. Nearly all impose a deadline for the ordering up of material. This is usually three-quarters of an hour prior to closing.

Conditions of admittance also vary. In most cases a temporary reader's ticket will be issued on the spot on production of suitable identification. A passport, a driving licence, a pension book or a cheque book and cheque guarantee card normally suffice.

Failure to produce at least one item of identification bearing your name, address and signature may result in non-admittance – and a wasted journey.

Certain County Records Offices now belong to the newly-instituted County Archive Research Network. In these cases tickets are generally issued for a four-year period. They allow the holder to use the facilities of all participating offices without the necessity of further registration. They do not, however, afford the right to preferential treatment either in the booking of seats or in the ordering up of material.

★   ★   ★

Before setting out for the County Records Office one should arm oneself with a pad of A4-size paper, plain or lined; several pencils (many CROs do not permit the use of pens); a pencil-sharpener, a rubber, and a stock of ten-pence coins – in case it is necessary to undertake any photocopying.

A magnifying glass can also prove surprisingly useful – even for those with perfect eyesight – not least when it comes to interpreting minute or faded writing or parchments where the language is archaic.

There is seldom any objection to pocket tape-recorders provided their use does not materially affect the concentration of other readers. As time spent in County Records Offices needs to be utilised to maximum advantage, tape-recorders are a helpful ancillary tool when it comes to gleaning material which cannot be photocopied – either owing to the restrictions of copyright or because it is too fragile to be completely opened up or bent back. Without a tape-recorder, this material will have to be laboriously copied out in longhand.

In some cases the problem can be surmounted by the use of a portable typewriter, but it is always best to check on its use in advance. Some institutions – such as the British Museum Newspaper Library at Colindale – provide sound-proofed booths for this purpose. In the absence of such a facility typewriters may be excluded entirely.

Most County Records Offices permit non-flashlight photography. This can usually be undertaken on the spot by the reader, using his own camera, in which case permission should be obtained from the archivist on duty.

Alternatively, readers can apply to have material reproduced through the CRO's own photographer. In this case a charge is levied. Readers are also expected to pay the cost of packing and postage. Delivery times vary from as little as five days to eight weeks, depending on the efficiency and workload of the CRO in question.

★   ★   ★

On arrival at the County Records Office, and having completed the registration formalities, you will be asked to sign the visitors' book. You will also be asked to enter your address and the broad nature of your enquiry.

My own experience has taught me that most archivists are both highly qualified and extremely knowledgeable. Provided you retain their goodwill – and they experience a surprising amount of rudeness at the hands of readers – they will become your most valuable allies. They have a natural enthusiasm for local history which extends well beyond the call of duty. It is quite possible that, having ordered up material, you will be re-approached by the archivist, half an hour later, with additional suggestions. I am constantly surprised and gratified by this readiness to go away and mull things over, to adopt readers' projects as their own.

★   ★   ★

Because the potential avenues of research are so numerous – in many cases more than thirty – it is essential to approach them in an orderly manner. Although circumstances will not always permit a rigid adherence to it, the list which follows offers the best chance of success.

Ordnance Survey Maps

The most common mistake made by first-time researchers – and unquestionably the most mortifying – is to find themselves investigating the wrong property. This is less likely to occur with an isolated farmhouse than with a terraced dwelling situated in a built-up area. Nonetheless, it has been known to happen.

It is therefore vital, at the very outset, to determine whether the property has ever been subject to renaming or renumbering; or whether the street in which it stands was formerly known by another name.

This is best done by reference to maps. All County Records Offices retain copies of Ordnance Survey maps. By examining these it should be possible to pinpoint the property fairly exactly. Some maps show the numbers or names of dwellings, others do not. Nonetheless, by working back through the years it should be possible to see whether the house, and where applicable the street, has ever been renumbered or renamed.

Some maps – the later ones, predominantly – are more detailed than others. Although cartographers are not immune to the temptations of artistic licence, they tend by and large to be accurate and conscientious recorders of fact.

On early maps, all but the grandest houses are usually shown as uniform squares, not unlike the property blocks used in Monopoly. On later ones they may be delineated individually and in some detail.

Where this is the case it is important to note the fact. Discrepancies in outline are a useful clue to structural alterations. However, where the outline is totally dissimilar we should remember that not every house shown on an early map is necessarily the building which occupies the site today.

Once having established that we are dealing with the right property –

and having made a note of the date of any change in name and street numbering (which should be picked up at the relevant time) we may safely return to the present. Having done so, we must turn to:

The Electoral Register

Although the layman often finds the idea preposterous, it is generally a great deal more difficult to uncover information about the occupant of a property in, say, 1975 than his counterpart of a century earlier. Much of the blame for this attaches to the ludicrous restraints of the Official Secrets Act; and to local government's love of bureaucracy.

For reasons of security, the street directories – a useful tool which we shall encounter next – ceased to publish the names of domestic residents much beyond the late 1960s.

The ten-yearly Census returns, which might otherwise prove invaluable, are subject to the Official Secrets Act and are therefore only released a hundred years after compilation. The next Census is due in 1991, when the 1891 returns will be released.

Modern rate-books are another source which ought to enable us to compile a list of owners down the years, but are in most cases beyond the reach of the researcher. When I asked why this was I was informed that they contained 'sensitive' information. On pressing further I was told that they contained details of defaulters. A suggestion that defaulters might have forfeited the right to sensitive treatment was rejected . . . as insensitive.

This only leaves the Electoral Registers, sometimes known as the Voters' Lists. As the name suggests, these catalogue every member of a household registered to vote. But the information is essentially sparse and it is almost impossible to differentiate between owners and domestics. One can occasionally hazard an opinion on the strength of names – for instance, a Christabel, a Napier, a Fiona or a Wriothesley is less likely to belong to the linen-scrubbing tribe than a Madge, a Bertha or a Gladys – but it remains little more than an educated guess.

An additional drawback is that the earliest Electoral Registers are restricted to lists of freeholders, the property-owning classes, then the only people with the right to vote. By the same token, women fail to appear on it until 1918, the year of their enfranchisement. Foreign nationals, of course, don't appear on it at all.

On a brighter note, it should be said that I have never encountered a case where all these problems coincided; and the registers do often provide invaluable information for the years when other records let us down.

All being well, we have now filled in the 'missing' years, and can turn our attention to a rather fatter source of information.

The Directories

The chief of these is *Kelly's Street Directory*, first produced in about 1840 and, although still going strong, effective for our purpose only until about 1970. Those for London, and other principal towns, list all the major streets situated reasonably close to the town centre. (There is usually a separate section for the suburbs.)

Kelly's lists streets alphabetically. Beneath the street heading, which is set in bold type, properties are catalogued by number, the name of the principal householder appearing alongside.

By combing the directories year by year it should be possible to compile a list of occupants back to about 1840. Reference to the 'Trades' and 'Classified' sections of the directories for the years of their occupation may also help us to learn something of their professions.

Where a property fails to appear in the directories for two or three years consecutively, it is possible that it was empty, either undergoing refurbishment or even rebuilding. Recourse to the maps may help to establish this.

Using *Kelly's* to research London properties is relatively easy. In the provinces it can sometimes prove more difficult. *Kelly's* provincial directories have not always survived in as great a number as those produced for London, and those which have may contain rather less information. However, many towns produced local directories of a similar nature which are of equal, and sometimes greater value.

Provided all goes well *Kelly's*, and the local directories, should enable us to compile a list of occupants back to at least the middle of the last century. Thereafter, we must turn for information to the:

Rate-Books

The majority of County Records Offices maintain a card-index system showing when areas were first rated. Given that sustained rate evasion is a near impossibility, the chances of a dwelling having existed unnoticed by tax-gatherers prior to the date of the first rating are very small. We have thus established a highly significant fact, albeit a negative one. We now know when the house was *not* in existence.

Rate-books from about the middle of the nineteenth century onwards are relatively easy to decipher. There is usually an index to streets at the beginning of each volume, and properties within streets are generally numbered. However, as one moves further back in time the information becomes more difficult to extract.

Part of the problem lies in the fact that the rate-books were never intended to be used as a historical source. They were simply utilitarian records of money-gathering.

In the seventeenth and eighteenth centuries the rate-collector wandered around in no very coherent manner, a quill pen in his hand and an inkpot at his lapel. He seldom bothered to note down the number of a property, only the payer's name. Entries were made with the book balanced on the collector's knee, propped up against a wall or, sometimes, on the householder's back. Streets were not always properly identified and the rate-books are full of such ambiguous headings as 'Across the way', or 'Up the Hill'.

The best hope of retracing the course of these long-dead collectors is by returning to the maps.

The absence of house-numbering is a more serious problem. It can usually be resolved, however, by working backwards through the years, using a chart similar to the one reproduced (opposite).

As can be seen, the first entry should be culled from the earliest street directory which lists dwellings by their individual numbers or names. By taking the names of, say, five householders on either side of the house in which we are interested – No. 74 in our example – it should be possible to move back through the uncharted territory of the rate-books, using our ten 'dummy' householders as bench-marks or anchors.

Although, with the passage of years, changes will occur, it is most unlikely that more than two or three of our eleven residents will vacate in the course of any one year. Thus a newcomer – including a newcomer to No. 74 – can easily be slotted into his rightful position.

In addition to helping establish when a property was first built, and the names of the occupants down the years, the rate-books also contain information regarding rateable values. Any marked increase in a rateable value over the course of a short period (say a year) indicates that the property has been extensively altered or even rebuilt. Its absence from the rate-books altogether also suggests rebuilding – or that it was empty. People often fell down on their payments and the side-margins of the rate-books are full of such comments as 'Run away'.

Where houses are sub-divided, or where two are joined into one, rate-books can be difficult to interpret. It is also important to remember that a person paying rates on a property is not necessarily the occupant. Because many houses were constructed as part of a speculative building development, the first name in the rate-book is sometimes that of the architect or builder.

Arranged along similar lines to the rate-books are:

Land Tax Returns

These are generally only of use where the name of the householder is already known. They may however, give some clue as to status. Hearth Tax details will reveal how many fireplaces there were in the property; and it can be interesting to compare this number with the number existing today. Obviously, the more hearths there were, the grander the house.

Example of a Rate-Book Mapping Chart

YEAR	No. 69.	No. 70.	No. 71.	No. 72.	No. 73.	No. 74.	No. 75.	No. 76.	No. 77.	No. 78.	No. 79.
1854 (Kelly's)	Robert Hibbs	James Rosser	Michael Bates	James Kidd	John Abbot	Abigail Hunt	Mrs Dawson	Mrs Trim	Albert Hams	Jonathan Jones	Alfred Matthews
1849	Robert Hibbs	James Rosser	Empty	Arthur Doone	John Abbot	Thomas Bristow	George Grimmer	Empty	Albert Hams	Edward Baxter	Alfred Matthews
1844	Robert Hibbs	James Rosser	Robert Shore	Arthur Doone	John Stringer	Thomas Bristow	George Grimmer	Mrs Bell	Albert Hams	Empty	Charles Fulkes
1840	Mrs Hibbs	James Rosser	Michael London	Empty	John Stringer	Peter Wallace	William Mossop	John Garrick	Albert Hams	David Fulkes	Charles Fulkes
1835	Mrs Hibbs	James Rosser	Michael London	George Fiddler	John Stringer	Empty	William Mossop	Fred Hardy	Albert Hams	David Fulkes	Martin Kirtle
1830	James Hibbs	Harold Harbert	Michael London	John Greenberg	Mrs Arthur	David Hall	Empty	Fred Hardy	Albert Hams	the Widow Mann	Martin Kirtle
1825	James Hibbs	Harold Harbert	Michael London	John Greenberg	Mrs Arthur	David Hall	Onslow Grimes	Mrs Grimes	Albert Hams	the Widow Mann	Franklin Joyce
1820	James Hibbs	Harold Harbert	Empty	Empty	Fred Arthur	David Hall	Empty	Empty	Albert Hams	Empty	the Widow Mann

Glebe Terriers

Glebe Terriers are inventories of land or other property belonging to the
church. They are usually held at the Diocesan Registry, but it is quite possible
that copies have been lodged at the County Records Office. They sometimes
make reference to building dates and alterations.

Cathedral Records

Similar to the Glebe Terriers, these are records of properties owned by the
Dean and Chapter of a cathedral. In addition to evidence of building dates and
alterations, they sometimes contain original leases, some of them on
parchment and some of them in Latin.

Title Deeds

Contemporary deeds are useful in providing names of owners which can be
checked against other sources. This can be a disappointing line of enquiry,
however, as many of the earliest deeds have been lost or destroyed.

Estate Records

Many of the great landowners such as the Dukes of Westminster in London or
the Lords Ilchester in Somerset maintained detailed estate records. These
are sometimes lodged in the County Records Office. Others may only be open
to inspection on written application to the relevant Estate Office. Permission
is seldom withheld unreasonably, although you may be required to pay a small
fee to cover the time of the estate clerk who will supervise your visit and fetch
up any relevant documents.

Estate records contain details of leases, rent-rolls, surveyors' reports
and valuations. They do not in all cases identify properties individually. This
can often be rectified by consulting estate maps.

Architects', Builders' and Surveyors' Records

Most records held by the above have not survived. Many were considered of
no historical importance and ultimately destroyed. However, where they have
been lodged at the County Records Office they can provide valuable
information regarding building dates, costs and design. If the name of the
architect is discovered it may be worthwhile approaching The Royal Institute
of British Architects for further information about him.

Tithe Maps

Ironically, most of the tools of modern-day historical research – the Domesday Book, tithe maps, rate-books, Manorial Rolls and tax returns – were never produced with history in mind at all. They were entirely concerned with the acquisition of money, most of it for the public exchequer.

Tithes – which required that a tenth part of the annual produce of land, cattle and other sources of wealth in a parish be given to the church – were typical of this. They were first introduced into England in the eighth century by Offa, the most powerful of the Saxon kings. In order that the authorities might have some record of those on whom the tithe could be levied, a series of maps was drawn up, showing their landholdings.

Shortly after Queen Victoria came to the throne (in 1837), the parish tithes were commuted to a fixed annual charge. In 1840, and in consequence of this, a tithe map was produced. This shows the land of the parish divided up into portions. Each of these portions is numbered. The number, which relates to the owner and sometimes the occupier, corresponds to a similar number on an accompanying list, known as the Tithe Apportionment. By marrying the two we are able to discover not only the amount of land which may have been associated with a dwelling but also something of the status of the owner and occupier. (They were not necessarily one and the same.)

The Court Rolls

Where Court Rolls exist in tandem with the tithe map, it is sometimes possible to trace the occupants of the house back to the date of its first building. As this represents a rare prize, we should look at the manorial system in a little detail.

In ancient times, a manor was an estate granted by the Crown, usually to reward the services of a prominent knight. Under the feudal system, it became the basic unit of land tenure. The estate became a manor as soon as the occupant let out portions to sub-tenants. In the Middle Ages these tenants held their land not for a fixed term of years but three 'lives' – or generations. The system survived, in diluted form, as late as the early 1920s.

Tenancies were known as 'copyhold', because details of them were *copied* into the accounts of the manor. These accounts were known as the Court Rolls. As each tenant died, and was succeeded by his heir – the next 'life' – this was entered in the rolls, as was any surrender of his copyhold interest.

The value of the Manorial Court Rolls is therefore obvious. For the amateur historian there is, however, one serious flaw. The earliest of them are written in Latin.

The Victoria County History

This is a continually updated multi-volume work, which catalogues the history of the counties, rather as the *Survey* does for London. It is unlikely that any of the County Records Offices will hold a full set, but they will certainly have a copy of the volume relating to their particular county. This will give details of the early development of the area. If the house under review is extremely ancient, or occupies an ancient site, it will probably receive a passing mention. If it is, (or was once), a manor house in its own right, it will be covered in more detail.

Other Topographical Works

Most County Records Offices maintain a collection of topographical books. It is always worth taking the most promising of these and looking through the indexes for suitable references.

Archaeological Sources

The Victoria County History gives some account of the area in pre-history along with any major archaeological finds. For further information it may be worth contacting your local museum. Where it is possible to determine outdoor congregating areas – such as a seat by a water-mill – it might be an idea to test the ground with a geiger counter, or by gently lifting the top soil.

Fire Insurance Plans

Where these have been deposited at the County Records Office they usually show a building's use, structural features and building materials. In the case of more important buildings they sometimes give the occupier's name.

Sales Catalogues

Where sales catalogues have survived they are of enormous benefit in supplying evidence of how a property was formerly disposed. They also give an insight into house prices of the day. If they incorporate details of house contents they can tell us a great deal about the owners and their life-styles. Because they were usually compiled with great meticulousness, they can be used to refurnish a property visually, room by room.

Borough Records

Although modern documents are generally retained by the municipality, many early borough records will have been deposited with the County Records Office for safekeeping. As boroughs often owned significant amounts of property, their records contain information of leases, rentals, surveys, plans and repairs. Many of these records stretch back to the sixteenth century. They may include Burgess Rolls and accounts, and more recent material such as details of the gas, water, electricity and railway companies.

Cuttings Files

Many CROs retain a newspaper cuttings file. This is a collection of items of local interest extracted over the years from newspapers and magazines. The quantity and quality varies enormously. The best of them, those built up over a number of years, will be very eclectic. They will include everything from reports of local fetes, drama societies and football clubs to thumbnail sketches of local dignitaries, accounts of hauntings, meetings of the parish council, weddings and – of course – details of houses and their occupants.

Census Returns

Most County Records Offices hold Census returns for their area. Properly interpreted, they are an extremely fertile source of information. I therefore propose to deal with them, separately, in the next chapter.

Card Indexes

The majority of CROs maintain several card-index systems. One will almost certainly be an alphabetical list of properties detailing anything known about them. A second may be an alphabetical list of the names of people who feature in such CRO documents as leases and wills. A third will probably catalogue illustrative material such as maps, prints, paintings and photographs.

In many cases there is also an information index. This is a record of previous enquiries made by members of the public, together with copies of the archivist's replies. It is always worth checking this index in order to discover whether anything is already known about the property being researched. I have not detailed it as a principal task because many people prefer to discover the information for themselves. In that event the information index is a useful form of confirmation.

★   ★   ★

Having checked out all the sources above, we should now have a comprehensive list of names – and very few gaps. However, although we may have gleaned a little information about these people – from the classified section of *Kelly's*, from sales particulars or notations in rate-books – they remain mostly skeletons. We must now look to see how we may best bring them back to life.

PART TWO

THE
PEOPLE

CHAPTER FIVE

Census Returns

Reading Between the Lines

C ensus returns represent one of the most fertile areas of research
available. The first Census was taken in 1831. They have been
taken at ten-yearly intervals ever since. Unfortunately, as we
have seen, they are subject to the Official Secrets Act. This
requires them to be kept under lock and key for a period of a hundred years.
Consequently, the only ones available to us are those taken between 1831 and
1881. The 1891 Census is due to be released in 1991.

Because the 1831 Census is purely statistical, from our point of view it
serves no useful purpose. The remaining five returns list the name, the age,
the marital status, the occupation, and the place of birth of every inhabitant of
a property. They also indicate his or her relationship to the head of the
household.

These facts are perhaps dry enough in themselves. Properly interpreted, they reveal more about the occupants than they would ever have
dreamed. In order to demonstrate this I have reproduced an entry, culled at
random, for a 'typical' lower-middle-class Victorian family living in London in
1871.

By dealing with each of them in turn I hope to build up a detailed picture
of their lives using no more than the information given and what may
reasonably be inferred from the balance of probabilities.

1871 Census

Name	Position	Age	Status	Occupation	Born
Nathan Box	Head	52	Married	Former Clerk in East India Company	Burford, Oxon
Emma Box	Wife	47	Married	Glover	Leafield, Oxon
Mary Box	Daughter	30	Single	Glover	Burford, Oxon
Jane Ash	Daughter	28	Married	None	St Giles-in-the-Fields
James Box	Son	25	Single	Trainee Stockbroker	St Giles-in the-Fields
Emma Ash	Grand-daughter	7	Single	Scholar	India
Eliza Ash	Grand-daughter	5	Single	Scholar	India
Chas. Ash	Grandson	5 months	Single		India
Ann Batt	Mother-in-law	82	Widow	Annuitant	Witney, Oxon
Fanny Ollerenshaw		17	Single	General Domestic	Unknown
Annie Grub		19	Single	Wet Nurse	Northampton

NATHAN BOX, the head of the family, was born in the small Cotswold town of Burford in 1819, four years after the battle of Waterloo. His Christian name suggests he came of Jewish stock, but this cannot be established from the information on the Census return alone. It might be possible to discover the truth by consulting the registers of baptism for Burford, lodged either with the vicar at Burford or with the Oxfordshire County Records Office.

If Nathan Box was baptized into the Church of England, the entry showing this would also reveal the names (and possibly the occupations) of his father and mother. From a knowledge of the area, I suspect Mr Box Senior was an agricultural labourer. Alternatively, he may have worked with sheep. Burford had been a noted wool town since the Middle Ages.

As Nathan's eldest child, Mary, was born in 1841, her father must – unless Mary was illegitimate – have married her mother some time prior to this. Contraception then being almost non-existent, Mrs Box probably fell pregnant within a year of the ceremony – which would therefore have taken place in 1840, when Nathan was 21.

As Mary's place of birth is given as 'Burford', we know that the young Mr and Mrs Box lived there at least for a time after their marriage, possibly with Nathan's parents. However, as the second child, Jane, lists her place of birth as the London parish of St Giles-in-the-Fields in 1843, we know that the family must have moved to the capital sometime between this date and the date of Mary's birth, two years earlier.

Under what circumstances, or exactly where they lived on first coming to London, we do not know – although we might find out by acquiring a copy of Jane's birth certificate because in registering the birth Nathan would have been required to give not only his address but his occupation.

Whatever his line of work, one doubts whether Nathan Box warmed to the area of St Giles. Much of it was then occupied by a maze of mean and narrow little alleys and courts known as a 'rookery' – so called from the tendency of rooks to congregate and nest-build together.

It would have been very different to Burford. Contemporary chroniclers tell us that the rookery of St Giles was inhabited by 'criminals and the Irish'; and that any chance observer strolling through it on a Sunday morning would have witnessed at least three fights – and probably have been drawn into two of them.

As Nathan's youngest son, James, was born in the parish of St Giles-in-the-Fields in 1846 we know the family was still living there at that date. At what point they moved away the Census returns do not determine.

Nor do we know at what date Nathan joined the East India Company. It was, however, a fairly eminent employer. Founded by Royal Charter in the reign of Queen Elizabeth, to promote the trade in spices with the East Indies, it ultimately acquired dominion over Bengal, where it established its own constitution and exercised a power greater than that of many governments. Although it always pretended that its primary purpose was commerce, and that government was merely a tiresome if inevitable consequence of that, in 1858 its rule was transferred to the Crown and the East India Company ceased to exist.

Depending upon Nathan Box's seniority, it might be possible to learn something of his work with the East India Company through Crown records lodged at the Public Records Office at Kew.

When the activities of the East India Company were terminated, Nathan Box was only 39. What work he took thereafter, or whether indeed he found work at all, we do not know.

Nor do we know where or when he died. It might be possible to establish this, as well as cause of death, and his occupation at the time of death, by searching the registers of the Office of Population Censuses and Surveys at St Catherine's House, Aldwych, concentrating on the years after 1871.

EMMA BOX, Nathan's wife, was born at Leafield in Oxfordshire in 1824. Leafield is no great distance from Burford, and it is possible that she and Nathan had known one another all their lives.

They married when Emma was about sixteen. As it was common for brides to marry in their own parish, a search of the Leafield marriage registers might provide the exact date. The entry would also give us the name and occupation of her father.

Five years younger than her husband, Emma bore Nathan at least three children in the space of five years. I say 'at least' because there may well have been more – either before, in between or after. The fact that the Census return of 1871 lists no other children does not mean they didn't exist. They may have left home by then: to join the army, to marry, or possibly to go into service. The child mortality rate was also very high.

From the presence on the 1871 Census of her mother, we know that Emma's maiden name was Batt.

Emma earned a living as a glover. If Nathan was a typical Victorian he would not have cared to have his wife work. But if he continued unemployed after the closing down of the East India Company the family was almost certainly hard-up. At least Emma's trade was not as demanding as some; and it probably allowed her to work from home.

MARY BOX, Nathan and Emma's eldest child, was born at Burford in 1841 during the period before the family moved to London. When the Census enumerator called in 1871 she was thirty years of age. As such, she was perilously close to being considered on the shelf. As she lists her occupation as 'glover', it is likely that she worked as an assistant to her mother.

JANE ASH, the couple's second daughter, was the first of the Box children to be born in London . . . at least to the best of our knowledge. Pregnancies then came thick and fast. Consequently it is not beyond the bounds of possibility that Emma had another child sometime between Mary's birth in 1841 and Jane's in 1843. If such a child did arrive, it had either died or left home by 1871, when it would have been 29.

When the Census enumerator called on the family in 1871 Jane was 28 years of age. Her status she gives as 'married'. Yet the returns do not list her husband.

As all three of her children are recorded as having been born in India, Mr Ash may conceivably have been a soldier or involved in some form of Colonial administration. As the eldest Ash child, Emma – probably named after her grandmother – was born in 1864, we know the family was based in India at that date. Indeed, as the youngest, Charles – who may have been named after his father – was also born in India as late as 1870, we know that Jane Ash must have returned to England either at the end of 1870 or the beginning of 1871.

Her reasons for doing so are not clear. It may be that she had accompanied her husband to England on a period of leave. In this case his absence from the Census returns might be explained by the fact that on the day of the enumerator's visit he had gone to visit his parents or was travelling on some other business. We don't know – and now will never know. There is a theory that all history is written down . . . somewhere . . . and that a failure to unearth it reflects a lack of conscientiousness on the part of the researcher. In fact, ninety per cent of all historical data has disappeared beyond recall.

There is also the possibility that Mrs Ash had returned to England without her husband. She may have done so as the result of a domestic dispute or simply to see her parents.

JAMES BOX, was, to the best of our knowledge, Nathan and Emma's only son. At the age of 25 he seems to be a fraction old to be still training as a stockbroker. That he is doing so at all implies a rise in family status. One wonders what sacrifices Nathan and Emma endured to help him on in life – and what later became of him. Stock Exchange records might throw some light on this.

EMMA, ELIZA AND CHARLES ASH, Nathan and Emma's grandchildren, would have introduced a lively note into the Box household. Emma and Eliza, the two eldest, are listed as 'scholars'. This simply means they were of school age. The very fact that they were being educated in England, even on a temporary basis, tends to confirm the theory that Mrs Ash and her husband were undergoing a bona fide separation.

It may be that Mrs Ash had returned from India following a quarrel. On the other hand she may simply have brought the children back to settle them into boarding schools. Given the state of her parents' finances it seems unlikely that she could have afforded to send them away to school without the financial assistance of her husband. More probably, they were being educated locally on a day basis. Whether Mrs Ash returned to India once they were settled, we do not know.

ANN BATT, born in 1789, the year of the French Revolution, was Emma Box's mother. A native of Witney, a bustling Oxfordshire market town, she would have lived most of her life at Leafield, the residence of her husband, where Emma was born to her when she was 35. In an age when families of ten or twelve were not uncommon, Ann Batt would almost certainly have had children prior to Emma. She may have gone on producing for about ten years after, into her mid-forties.

If this was so, one wonders why, when her husband died, none of those offspring living locally offered Ann Batt a home. As she lists her occupation as 'annuitant', she would not have been a burden. The term 'annuitant' means that she was in receipt either of some form of pension – possible relating to the occupation of her late husband – or an income deriving from investments.

It says much for Nathan Box's charity that he was prepared to give his mother-in-law a home . . . although she no doubt contributed to the household expenses.

FANNY OLLERENSHAW, the Boxs' seventeen-year-old general domestic, lists her place of birth as 'unknown'. It may be that she belonged to a family of itinerant traders who travelled the country. It may be that she was an orphan. Her name suggests a northern origin, but one cannot be sure.

As the only permanent domestic catering to the needs of a family of nine, Fanny Ollerenshaw's life would have been hard. She would have risen before dawn to tote in the coals and light the fires. She would then have helped Emma Box and her daughters make the beds, scrub the kitchen floor and front steps, dust, clean and polish. She would have been kept on the go well into the evening, perhaps snatching a break in the middle of the afternoon to peruse the latest copy of the *Servant's Journal* – the Victorian equivalent of the *Sun*.

ANNIE GRUB, the last of the names to appear on the Census return for 1871, seems to have been a sad case. She was employed as a wet-nurse, almost certainly for Jane Ash's youngest child, Charles, aged five months. She must therefore have recently had a child of her own. But this child does not appear on the Census returns. As Annie lists her status as 'single', it must have been illegitimate.

Annie had clearly become embroiled in a love affair. This may have been in her native Northampton. On the other hand she may have been in service in some other part of the country, in which case her lover would most likely have been one of the other servants – or even her employer. What is not in dispute is that she produced a child.

It may have been stillborn or she may have farmed it out, possibly to her parents. She seems then to have come to London in a pathetic effort to secure a few months' board and lodging in exchange for her breast milk, the birthright of her own child.

In most Victorian households, Annie Grub would have been discharged as soon as her milk dried up. Nathan Box had already demonstrated a degree of charity towards his mother-in-law. One hopes he was similarly disposed towards his grandson's unfortunate wet-nurse.

★ ★ ★

The immense amount of detail revealed by this single entry in the Census returns for 1871 is a graphic illustration of what may be learned from a close study of one document . . . provided one has the wit to see it.

Occasionally – very occasionally – it is possible to dredge up a fact so bizarre that it almost defies belief.

In 1986 I was commissioned to research the history of Beltone Court, a Victorian farmhouse in Somerset. In the course of the work I looked out the Census returns for 1861. Here I found a family named Vincent living in one of the farm outbuildings. James Vincent was an agricultural labourer employed by the farm bailiff. Among his children was a little girl named Sophie, aged two.

A year later, I was researching another property, a large mansion block in London's 'Little Venice', when, in perusing the Census returns for 1881 I came across an entry which made my blood run cold. It gave details of a young woman employed in the household as a parlourmaid. Her name was Sophie Vincent. Her age was 22, and she gave as her place of birth the small Somerset hamlet which I had been researching.

As the hamlet surrounding Beltone Court then boasted a population of less than a hundred souls, there could be no doubt that the two-year-old moppet of 1861 and the 22-year-old London parlourmaid were one and the same. I asked a friend, a professional statistician, to compute the odds of unearthing a curiosity of this nature. They are several million to one.

Why Sophie Vincent's name should have stuck in my mind from the original commission, I cannot say.

Helping the Dead to Speak

Armed with our list of occupants, and the additional information gleaned from the Census returns, we can now go to a number of standard works of biographical reference. Most of these sources will be found in major reference libraries. Some will also be carried by the County Records Office.

The Dictionary of National Biography

This is a work of many volumes, with subject entries arranged alphabetically. It lists most British men and women of note up to the end of the last century. There are several supplementary volumes covering the years from 1901. As the latest of these carries a cumulative index it is not necessary to search through all the later volumes individually when looking for a name. However, when the name being followed up is a relatively common one it is necessary to exercise great care. Most of these precautions are elementary. In the first flush of excitement, they are sometimes overlooked.

For instance, where the list of house occupants includes the name of a James Makepeace, and where the *Dictionary of National Biography* carries an entry for a similarly-named individual, they may well be one and the same man. But if the Makepeace noticed by the *DNB* is shown to have lived a hundred years before – or to have spent his entire life chasing butterflies in the Australian outback – we may be sure that they are not.

Entries are usually extremely comprehensive. Like the famous Mr Toad, the *DNB* 'knows all there is to be knowed'. As happens with modern-day *Times* obituaries, the entries were frequently written by people who had known the subject well. Common to many Victorian publications, the style is sometimes verbose but the information is impeccable.

A typical entry will list the subject's antecedents, his early career, his progressive rise and his death. There will then follow a general assessment of his or her character, together with any amusing little anecdotes that have survived. A final paragraph, italicized and in parentheses, lists any books written either by or about the subject.

This final paragraph will also give details of any surviving portraits. However, these may now prove difficult to locate. A sketch of a subject, said by the *DNB* to be 'in the collection of the late gentleman's grandson at Wittering Manor', may now be almost anywhere. On the other hand, illustrative material noted as being in the hands of the National Portrait Gallery or other recognized institutions, will probably prove relatively easy to find and, if necessary, to have reproduced.

Who Was Who

When people listed in *Who's Who* die, their entries are removed and entombed in *Who Was Who*. The volumes of *Who Was Who* cover the period from the turn of the century to the present day. There is a separate cumulative index, so it is not necessary to search every volume.

Unlike the *DNB* and the obituaries carried by *The Times* – which we shall discuss next – entries in *Who Was Who* tend to be restricted to a rather dull catalogue of official posts and offices held, unredeemed by anecdote. However, such entries do provide the framework of a life.

In order to demonstrate how they can be expanded from the basic telegramese – without deviating from the facts – I include a paraphrasing of the life of James Halpin, whose official *Who Was Who* entry, on which it is based, appears opposite. The only information not culled from Halpin's entry in *Who Was Who* is that concerning the wholesale eviction of Irish tenants by their British landlords, which is the result of additional research.

Born in the summer of 1843, James Halpin was a fiery Irish Nationalist. He was educated firstly at Newmarket on Fergus National School, then at Springfield College, Ennis.

In 1888, when 44 years old – an age when many of his political contemporaries had settled for expressing dissent rather less dramatically – Halpin greeted the release from prison of a prominent Irish Nationalist by setting off fireworks. Ironically, the escapade terminated in his own imprisonment. While the experience was no doubt not pleasant, he returned to his Nationalist activities unchastened.

HALPIN, James, M.P. (Nat.) West Clare from 1906; *b.* June 1843; *s.* of William Halpin. *Educ.:* Newmarket on Fergus National School; Springfield College, Ennis. Was in every National movement from 1859, viz. The Phœnix, The Fenian, Land League, National League, and United Irish League; in the spring of 1888 sent to jail for letting off fireworks in honour of Mr. O'Brien's release from prison; presided at the great Land League demonstration at Ennis, for which was sent to Hotel Balfour at Limerick for three months; had to try to sleep on the plank bed for first month, also to break stones into gravel for same period; always a supporter of C. S. Parnell; took part in all the elections in support of Mr. W. H. K. Redmond for East Clare; President of the East Clare Executive U.I.L.; member Clare County Council and Clare County Board Gaelic League; Hon. Sec. Corid Caitlin Branch Gaelic Athletic Association League; prosecuted and brought to the Cork Winter Assizes for organising erection of evicted tenants' huts; hated to be in a British Parliament, but hoped to see the day when Irishmen would be allowed to make their own laws in their own land; Poor Law Guardian Ennis Union from 1880 to 1895; Chairman of it for three years; opposed the late Lord Inchiquin as Chairman, and after five years' fight put him out; was contractor, and completed Lehinch Sea Wall, by which he lost £500; was a large farmer; erected and owned the Fergus Vale Creamery. *Recreations:* rowing, cycling, walking; one of the fours who won the Ennis Cup for rowing at the Clan Castle Regatta in 1877-1878. *Address:* Newmarket on Fergus. *Clubs:* Dailgais Athletic, Commercial and Abbey, Ennis; Limerick and Clare Farmers'.

Died 26 July 1909.

After presiding over the great Land League demonstrations at Ennis, Halpin was again locked up, this time for three months. The authorities appear to have taken a dim view of this second offence because for the first month he was required by day to break rocks and to sleep at night on a wooden plank – treatment usually reserved for criminal prisoners sentenced to terms of hard labour.

A political creature through and through, Halpin is said to have 'hated to be in a British parliament'. Nonetheless, like Charles Parnell, whom he supported, he suffered it as the only means of furthering the cause of Irish Nationalism. He was in every National movement from 1859 including the Phoenix, the Fenian, the Land and National Leagues and the United Irish League.

His third appearance in a court of law was at the Cork Winter Assizes where he was charged with erecting makeshift huts to house Irish tenants evicted from their pitiful hovels by their English masters.

Some of these, like the infamous Lord Lucan, the inept commander of the Heavy Brigade at Balaclava, considered the Irish sub-human . . . and treated them accordingly.

When he decided that agriculture was less profitable than the rearing of sheep, Lord Lucan embarked on a policy of wholesale eviction. When his estate workers found that they could not demolish the flimsy structures of the peasants fast enough to please his Lordship, Lucan commissioned the construction of a machine which would do the job at three times the speed.

In this manner, thousands of people were rendered homeless. Their smallholdings were allowed to revert to pastureland. The dispossessed were left to starve and die in the nearest ditch. (As a Poor Law Guardian, Lord Lucan had no intention of allowing them to clutter up the workhouse and took delight in turning them away personally.) He and his policies are generally thought to have been responsible for at least thirty thousand Irish deaths.

On one occasion, thinking him safely in London, a group of Lord Lucan's tenants gathered in the market square and burned him in effigy. His Lordship suddenly galloped down on them, the hooves of his snorting black steed striking sparks from the cobblestones, and screamed: 'I'll evict the lot of you!'

In the light of this, the opposition of James Halpin, and that of men like him becomes eminently understandable. Halpin never ceased from the struggle. As he said himself, he only lived 'to see the day when Irishmen would be allowed to make their own laws in their own land . . .'

Ironically, like Lord Lucan, Halpin was also a Poor Law Guardian. Unlike Lucan he believed the workhouse should be a sympathetic refuge for the destitute, not a surrogate form of imprisonment.

His predecessor as Chairman of the Guardians of the Ennis workhouse, Lord Inchiquin, was a hard-liner in the Lucan mould. Halpin unseated him after a fight lasting five years. All in all, he served as a Poor Law Guardian for fifteen years from 1880 to 1895, the last three of them as Chairman.

Although Halpin owned the local dairy, the Fergus Vale Creamery – and although he farmed large estates at Newmarket on Fergus, the town of his birth – he was careful to reinvest money in the community. He it was who built the sea wall at Lehinch – 'by which he lost £500'.

A keen sportsman, who won the Ennis Cup for rowing at the Clan Castle Regatta in 1877, James Halpin never forgot his early roots or loyalties. He continued to retain a house at Newmarket on Fergus until his death, which occurred on 26 July 1909, about a month after his sixty-sixth birthday.

★   ★   ★

The date of death which *Who Was Who* furnishes for subjects at the end of each entry leads us on to the next source of reference:

Times Obituaries

The Times is the country's oldest surviving national daily newspaper. More importantly, it is the only one covered by a comprehensive index. This can be found in major reference libraries and is contained in bound quarterly volumes. Having culled the date of death from *Who Was Who*, we should now search the relevant index of *The Times* to see whether our subject merited a mention. In the event that he did, the entry will read something as follows:

Makepeace, R. 18j 7a.

The figure 18 represents the date, while the letter *j* denotes the month of the entry. (Although *j* could represent either January, June or July, the volumes of the index are so disposed that no two months beginning with the same letter ever fall within the same quarterly volume.)

The second numeral is the page number on which the obituary can be found, and the letter *a* indicates that it begins in the first column. (If it began in the second or third columns the last reference would be *b* or *c*.)

The Times obituaries are useful for several reasons. Although they nearly always contain the information listed in the subject's entry in *Who's Who*, they are generally supplemented by anecdote and reminiscences supplied by the obituarist, who often knew the subject well. The obituaries of more prominent individuals may be graced by a photograph.

In some instances there will be several entries. Where the news of a death reaches the newspaper too late to include a full obituary this will take the form of a brief notice on the front page. It will be followed – usually the next day – by a larger piece.

In the days that follow various chums will probably write to *The Times* with 'appreciations'. If these are published they, too, will appear in the index. The authors of appreciations are usually identified only by their initials.

Details of any memorial service will also be shown. Although the list of guests attending these is very densely printed and therefore tiresome to read, the effort should be made. Memorial services can be invaluable in providing clues to the subject's business activities and social interests. On several occasions I have found the name of a subject's mistress . . . who no doubt slipped into a rear pew at the last moment, incognito.

Finally, it is always advisable to search two or sometimes three volumes beyond the last reference to a subject for mention of a will. A complicated one may remain in probate for at least six months.

Wills

Wills serve a very special purpose. Although we are all interested to know how much money a man makes, the amount he leaves can be a far sharper guide to his character. For instance, the extrovert W. S. Gilbert, the librettist of the Savoy Operas, left a great deal more than his staid and sober-minded partner, Sir Arthur Sullivan.

When we consider how much information is needlessly denied us by the Official Secrets Act, it is quite astounding that anyone can apply for a copy of anyone else's birth certificate and anyone can obtain a copy of a probated will.

In the latter case it is only necessary to search the yearly volumes of the indexes lodged with the Principal Registry of the Family Division of Somerset House and pay a fee of 25 pence. You will not be asked for identification nor the purpose for which you require the document. Because there are many searchers and space is limited, you may only make short extracts in pencil. However, copies of wills may be ordered at a cost of 25 pence a page. These can either be collected or sent to you by post.

Wills provide details of bequests, and some of the items subject to these, such as family portraits, can often be traced. Wills of calculated spite are unusual, though not rare. They provide a curious insight into family relationships.

Institutions, Specialist Publications and Other Useful Books

Details of members of the clergy can be found in past and present editions of *Crockfords*. For information on members of the legal profession it is often worth writing to the Law Society. Members of the armed forces are covered by the Army & Navy lists. The Imperial War Museum may also be of help.

A good dictionary of architects is a glaring lack; but the Royal Institute of British Architects may have some biographical information regarding members past and present. There are several dictionaries of British artists and sculptors. I especially recommend Rupert Gunnis's *Dictionary of British Sculptors* (Abbey Library). The more important physicians and surgeons are mentioned by Reginald Pound in his excellent book *Harley Street* (Michael Joseph, 1967).

The follies and foibles of the British aristocracy have been wonderfully catalogued by E. S. Turner in *Amazing Grace: The Great Days of Dukes* (Michael Joseph, 1975). The *Complete Peerage* offers a more sober assessment, although the footnotes often contain forthright comments, culled from contemporary memoirs, regarding aristocratic weaknesses. Although only a relatively small proportion of houses will ever have had a member of the peerage as a tenant, many more will have formed part of an aristocratic estate. Some mention of the family is therefore essential.

Well-known music hall artistes will probably feature in standard works of biographical reference. The less famous may have merited inclusion in

Gammond's *Your Own, Your Very Own* (Ian Allan, 1971); or W. Macqueen-Pope's *Ghosts and Greasepaint,* (Hale, 1951). J. R. Taylor's *Dictionary of the Theatre,* (Penguin, 1966) may also be of use.

Those wishing to understand something of the servant way of life should read Horn's *The Rise and Fall of the Victorian Servant* (Gill & Macmillan, 1975); and E. S. Turner's very entertaining *What The Butler Saw: Two Hundred and Fifty Years of The Servant Problem* (Michael Joseph, 1962).

Who Was Who frequently lists the clubs to which subjects belonged. For further information on clubs and clubmen I recommend Lejeune and Lewis's *The Gentlemen's Clubs of London* (Macdonald and Janes, 1979); R. H. Nevill's *London Clubs* (Chatto & Windus, 1947); and (particularly) Tom Girtin's *The Abominable Clubman* (Hutchinson, 1964).

Subjects known – or thought – to be still living, may merit an entry in the current volume of *Who's Who.* This will probably supply a home address and telephone number.

Failing an entry in *Who's Who,* a check should be made to see whether there is a listing for them in the local telephone directory. Former occupants can often supply personal information about their predecessors which can be doubly valuable as there is seldom a written record of it. By the same token, it is always worth talking to neighbours, as well as other people who have lived in the vicinity for any length of time.

Compiling a Family Tree

For many people it is sufficient to learn something of the lives of previous owners during the period of their occupancy. However, research can be both infinite and deeply addictive. Those who wish to carry the study a step further may want to construct a family tree.

Unless the family is one's own – when it is best to start by talking to relatives – the first source for this is the evidence contained in:

Certificates of Birth, Death & Marriage at St Catherine's House

From 1 July 1837 all this information was collated under one roof by the Registry of Births, Deaths and Marriages at Somerset House. It is now lodged at St Catherine's House, Aldwych, London. In most cases it is therefore relatively easy to trace a family back to the beginning of the reign of Queen Victoria.

The search rooms at St Catherine's House are divided into three separate areas, one each for births, deaths and marriages. Each section contains rows of steel shelves accommodating large bound volumes. In the births section each volume contains details of all births sent to the Registrar during the course of one quarter. The volumes cover the periods January to March; April to June; July to September; and October to December.

Unless a searcher has a fairly accurate idea of a subject's date of birth, it will be necessary to make a rough calculation, working through the years either side. This can involve searching through a large number of volumes. They are heavy and cumbersome.

Owing to the public's new-found absorption with tracing its antecedents, there is not always a counter on which to rest the books, because the search rooms become extremely crowded. It is therefore a good idea to get to St Catherine's House as soon as it opens. Although it is bad at most times of the day, the press tends to be acute between noon and 2 p.m. Although it can be irritating to have to elbow one's way through a solid mass of people in this manner, it is profoundly satisfying to see so many of them giving up their lunch-hour in order to learn more about their roots.

If you are unable to attend at St Catherine's House in person, you may apply by post requesting staff to undertake a search on your behalf. However, the fee is ten pounds and restricted to a period of five years. This charge equates to fifty pence a volume. It is therefore preferable, where it can be arranged, to have a friend undertake the research for you.

At St Catherine's House, as elsewhere, you get what you pay for. There is no charge for people wishing to research the indexes in person. But the indexes themselves contain no detailed information, merely a reference consisting of the registration district, the volume and the page number, relating to a specific birth. In case there is more than one entry for the same name, it is as well to have at least some idea of the likely registration district.

It should also be remembered that the date shown in the index is the date of registration, *not* of birth. Consequently a child born on 31 December 1858 will appear in the first quarter for 1859. The same holds good for marriages and deaths. The exact date will only appear on the certificate.

Once the subject's entry has been located, it is necessary to note the reference number on an application form and take it, together with the fee of five pounds, to the cashier. Your application for a full birth certificate – abbreviated ones are of little use for our purposes – will be receipted and a copy of the certificate will be left at the Collections Desk for you some time after three o'clock two days later. If collected in person, it will only be released on production of a receipt. Alternatively, it can be forwarded by post.

The data given in full birth certificates include: when and where a child was born; the name, if any; the sex; the name and surname of the father; the name, and surname and maiden name of the mother; the occupation of the father; the signature, description and residence of the person laying the information before the Registrar (usually one of the parents); the date of registration; the signature of the Registrar; and any name which may have been entered after the registration.

Marriage certificates provide evidence of where and when a couple married; their names and ages; their condition – i.e. bachelor or widower, spinster or widow; their rank or profession; their residence at the time of the marriage; and the names, surnames and rank or profession of both fathers.

It is easier to locate a marriage through the Registry indexes than a birth

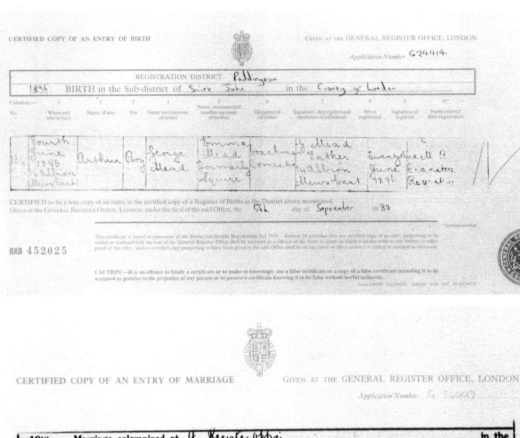

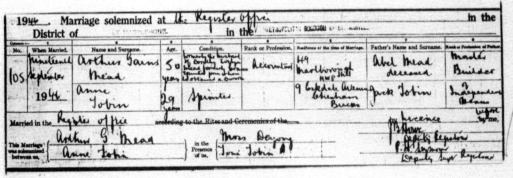

because the names of both parties appear separately. Both names should be checked, the least common first. If the index references are identical, the case is proven, and the certificate can be applied for with relative confidence.

Death certificates give details of the place where the subject died; the sex; age; occupation; and cause of death. They also supply the signature, the description and residence of the person informing the Registrar of the death

Application Number G 24414

QDX 07461£

CERTIFIED COPY OF AN ENTRY

CAUTION:—It is an offence to falsify a certificate or to make or knowingly use a false certificate or a copy of a false certificate intending it to be accepted as genuine to the prejudice of any person or to possess a certificate knowing it to be false without lawful authority.

DEATH | Entry No. | 9

Registration district　St. Marylebone

Administrative area
City of Westminster

Sub-district　North West Marylebone

1. Date and place of death　*J.l.t April 1969*
72. Carlton Hill. St. Maryle.

2. Name and surname　*Arthur Gains MEAD*

3. Sex　*Male*

4. Maiden surname of woman who has married

5. Date and place of birth　*Thirtyfirst March 1896.*
Chesham Buckinghamshire.

6. Occupation and usual address
Accountant
72. Carlton Hill Westminster

7.(a) Name and surname of informant
Ann Mead

(b) Qualification
Widow of deceased

(c) Usual address
72. Carlton Hill N.W.8.

8. Cause of death
I (a) Heart Failure
(b) Coronary Thrombosis
(c) Generalised Arteriosclerosis
II Cerebro-vascular disease.
certified by
John Horder　B.M.

9. I certify that the particulars given by me above are true to the best of my knowledge and belief
Signature of informant

10. Date of registration　*Fifth April 1969*

11. Signature of registrar　*BJHerod Deputy Registrar.*

CERTIFIED to be a true copy of an entry in the certified copy of a register of Deaths in the District above mentioned. Given at the GENERAL REGISTER OFFICE, LONDON, under the Seal of the said Office on *5th* **September** **1988**

This certificate is issued in pursuance of the Births and Deaths Registration Act 1953. Section 34 provides that any certified copy of an entry purporting to be sealed or stamped with the seal of the General Register Office shall be received as evidence of the birth or death to which it relates without any further or other proof of the entry, and no certified copy purporting to have been given in the said Office shall be of any force or effect unless it is sealed or stamped as aforesaid.

(usually the family doctor); the date the death was registered; and the signature of the Registrar.

Unlike birth and marriage certificates, which provide details of subjects' parents, death certificates are only of use in fleshing out the facts – such as where and from what a subject died. The age, however, is generally accurate and does allow us to compute a date of birth.

With each certificate costing five pounds – and one may need many of them in order to trace a family back to 1837 – genealogy is an expensive hobby. It is, however, intensely rewarding. In order to minimize the cost and avoid the ordering up of irrelevant certificates, it is vital, as in every other area of research, to start from a solid foundation – that which one *knows* to be true.

★ ★ ★

Having obtained all the necessary information back to 1837 from St Catherine's House, the next source of information is the:

Parish Registers

These are generally cheaper to research than the indexes at St Catherine's House, but the information is often catalogued in an irregular manner – especially prior to 1754. Much depends on the conscientiousness of the vicar.

Some registers have births, deaths and marriages on the same page, sometimes they are interspersed.

For many years, all back registers were kept in the parish, usually in a safe in the church vestry. There is now a more enlightened policy whereby all but the current registers may be deposited for safe-keeping with the local Records Office. Most incumbents have chosen to take advantage of this. However, it is important to remember that in a village with a tiny population, registers may take several generations to fill.

Where it is necessary to search registers held in the parish, remember that vicars are very busy people. They may not always be instantly available. Parish registers are valuable official documents. Consequently, incumbents may want to supervise the search, usually remaining in sight if not within earshot. They do not charge for their time, but there is an unwritten rule that researchers make a contribution to church funds. Except in the case of dire poverty, this should not be less than three pounds. Five pounds is normal, more will be considered generous. Only the insensitive allow the mission's success or failure to determine the size of the donation.

In the case of the register of baptisms, the information can vary considerably. It may simply give the name and date of baptism of the child. In most cases the names of the parents appear, sometimes also the father's occupation.

Prior to 1812, entries were made on blank leaves on a line-by-line basis. After 1812 the pages were divided into eight printed sections, each one with spaces for a child's Christian name, the Christian and surnames of its parents, the father's occupation and address, and the name and signature of the vicar officiating at the ceremony.

It should be noted that the dates given are not those of birth but of *baptism*. The two were not usually very different but there are frequent cases of conscience-stricken parents baptizing their sometimes quite mature brood *en masse*.

Until 1753, marriage registers also consisted of blank pages. Thereafter they were printed, with spaces for the names of the parties, their status, the parishes from which they came, whether they were of 'full' age (i.e. over 21) and the occupation of the groom. Entries were signed by both parties as well as two witnesses and the officiating minister. Those who were illiterate made their mark, usually in the form of a cross. Witnesses were often related to the bride and groom.

Prior to the late Victorian era, when illiteracy was widespread, many names were written down phonetically, as verbalized to the minister at the altar. Thus, when researching a family with a name capable of variation, such as Parsloe, entries written as 'Parslo' or 'Parslow' should also be taken into account. It doesn't automatically follow that they are one and the same – but the chances are high.

Until the second decade of the nineteenth century, burial entries tended to be written in short-form, giving only the name (and sometimes the age) of the deceased. After that, printed pages were introduced and these give more information, such as place of abode, date of burial, and the name of the minister officiating.

From 1678 until the relevant parliamentary Act was repealed in 1814, it was decreed that 'no corpse or any person (except those who shall die of the plague) shall be buried in any shirt, shift sheet or shroud . . . other than what is made of sheep's wool only'.

This was a blatant and partisan attempt to further the interests of the wool trade, on which the country's rural economy was based. Penalties for non-compliance were draconian.

In Scotland, parish registers were kept on a less satisfactory basis. Much of the information contained in English registers is missing. There are no County Records Offices, but those registers surviving have been deposited at New Register House in Edinburgh. They may be consulted for a fee of £4.50 a day.

Where families remained static over many generations, it is sometimes possible to trace them back through the registers of a single parish to the day when those records were first kept. This is every genealogist's dream – but it seldom happens.

In most cases there are simply too many gaps and ambiguities. People tended to move around from parish to parish in search of work. The more indigent were subject to the Poor Law. This meant that any newcomers to a village were watched like a hawk for the first year and a day because if they looked like becoming a burden on the parish during this period they could be returned to their former one. After that, their new parish became responsible for them.

Where a family disappears from one set of registers, it is sometimes possible to pick them up by searching through the registers of the surrounding parishes. In an age before the widespread introduction of public transport, people may have moved . . . but they seldom moved very far. However, as the net is spread ever wider the task becomes harder and the chances of a

successful trace begin to decrease. Beyond a certain point, the game ceases
to be worth the candle; and – unless one is prepared to search through every
parish register in the country – one is forced to face the fact that the trail has
gone cold.

Bishops' Transcripts

In the autumn of 1538 Thomas Cromwell, Henry VIII's Vicar-General, issued
a directive ordering that every parish in the land should record details of all
births, deaths and marriages occurring within its boundaries. At the end of
each year a transcript had to be sent to the bishop under pain of penalty. The
benefit of such transcripts to the modern historian is that they have often
survived where the original parish registers have perished.

Non-Conformist Records

Amateur genealogists tend to assume that their ancestors were baptized into
the Church of England. When they are unable to locate them in the parish
registers, they are frequently nonplussed. Their research consequently
grinds to a halt. They seldom consider the possibility that their ancestors may
have been nonconformists.

Members of the Roman Catholic faith are detailed in documents held by
the local County Records Office. The Catholic Record Society also possesses
much valuable information although it will not, generally, undertake research.

Baptist records are somewhat sparse. Details can be obtained through
the Baptist Historical Society based at the Baptist Union Library, 4
Southampton Row, London WC1B 4AB.

The library of the United Reformed Church Historical Society, also
based in Bloomsbury at 86 Tavistock Place, London WC1H 9RT, holds details
of the Congregational Church of England and Wales, and the Presbyterian
Church of England, united in 1792. Written enquiries are dealt with on a
first-come-first-served basis by a body of volunteer researchers. (All written
enquiries, to whatever source, should always be accompanied by a stamped
addressed envelope.) The library is open to visitors, generally by appointment, on Tuesday, Thursday and Friday of each week between 10.30 a.m.
and 4 p.m. It houses more than six thousand books and two thousand
pamphlets.

Registers containing details of Congregationalists (or Independents) are
housed in the old Congregational Library at 14 Gordon Square, London
WC1H 0AG.

Information on Quakers, who tend to have kept scrupulous records, is
kept at the Library of The Society of Friends, Euston Road, London
NW1 2BJ.

Since the seventeenth century, Jews have migrated to England in great
number. They fall into two categories: Sephardic Jews from Italy, Spain and
Portugal; and Ashkenazi Jews from the countries of Eastern Europe and

Holland. The principal sources of information regarding them are the Jewish Historical Society, based at 33 Seymour Place, London W1H 5AP; the Jewish Museum, Woburn House, Upper Woburn Place, London WC1H 0EP; and the local synogogue.

Methodists – who separated from the Church of England during the lifetime of John Wesley (1703–1791) – established chapels known as 'preaching houses'. The earliest Methodist registers date from 1795. However, as schisms developed and members transferred from one chapel to another, records became confused. Consequently, it can be difficult to maintain a thread of continuity.

The International Genealogical Index

From a belief that all life – past, present and future – is part of a continuing process, the (Mormon) Church of Jesus Christ of Latter Day Saints, based at Salt Lake City, Utah, USA, has undertaken a massive programme of computerised research. The result is the International Genealogical Index (known as the IGI). It contains more than eighty million names, arranged alphabetically. Most County Records Offices have indexes of this, although they are mostly restricted to the index for their own county.

The Society of Genealogists

Based at 14 Charterhouse Buildings, Goswell Road, London EC1M 7BA, the Society has a comprehensive collection of records, including copies of a great number of parish registers. Those wishing to undertake protracted research are strongly advised to become members. The charges to non-members are very reasonable and based on hourly, half-day or full-day research.

Other Parish Records

Until the Poor Law Reform Act of 1834, responsibility for the relief of the poor rested entirely with the parish. From the beginning of the seventeenth century it was the practice for a parish to nominate several Overseers of the Poor. These were usually churchwardens or other people prominent in village life. It was the Overseers' task to collect taxes in order to deal with the relief of the poor. The details of this earliest form of supplementary benefit are logged in three volumes: the Overseers' Accounts; the Churchwardens' Accounts; and the Poor Rate Book. Together they form what W. E. Tate in his book *The Parish Chest* called 'the intimate connection between the parish and the poor'.

The Poor Rate Book is a list of financial contributors. As not everyone in a village could afford to pay, it is also a roll-call of the affluent. The Overseers' Accounts give details of money dispensed to the poor – for food, for rent, for clothing, for medicines, for funeral expenses – as do the Churchwardens' Accounts.

Together, all three provide a wealth of ancillary information and are proof of the wisdom of researching the records of a parish in depth, not merely the parish registers.

Churchyards and Cemeteries

These provide useful sources of supplementary information, although they should be treated with caution. Dates on tombstones are not always reliable; and as they were often erected as memorials it doesn't automatically follow that all those listed on them are buried there. Nonconformist cemeteries evolved in the seventeenth century. The most famous is London's Bunhill Fields. Although there were public cemeteries in London by 1827, they did not become popular nationwide until the 1850s.

Most cemeteries have well-indexed records. These are usually lodged at the gate-house. They give the name, the age, address and occupation of the deceased. Entries in the records are normally preceded by a grave number. The precise location of the grave can usually be determined by looking up the number on a map of the cemetery, also held at the gate-house.

Other Sources

It is as well to remember, before setting out on research, that substantial pedigrees of families already exist. There are a number of useful examples in Burke's *Peerage* and Burke's *Landed Gentry*. Many printed pedigrees are included in the volumes below, the years covered being set in brackets:

G. W. Marshall: *The Genealogist's Guide* (to 1903), publ. Heraldry Today, 1903

J. B. Whitmore: *A Genealogical Guide*, publ. John Whitehead & Son Limited (1900-1950)

G. B. Barrow: *The Genealogist's Guide*, publ. Research Publishing Company, 1977 (1950-1977)

Finally, at the various stages of compiling a family tree it is important to stop and consider how the next gap may best be filled, drawing on the evidence already gleaned. Above all be honest. Record facts accurately and without glossing over indiscretions. They are the stuff of which history is made.

Remember, also, when writing the history of your house, to include some account of yourself. You're a part of it too.

PART THREE

PULLING IT ALL TOGETHER

A Suburban Villa

The White House
Kenley
Surrey

S ituated a little to the west of the busy A22, between Purley and Caterham, the village of Kenley stands at the heart of what is now London's southern dormitory belt. One says 'village', yet the place has no rural atmosphere. Nor is it a town. It exists in a form of limbo, somewhat between the two, a limbo known as suburbia.

It was only as I left the commercial area behind and began the ascent up Kenley Lane that the character of the neighbourhood changed. The houses grew larger. Some were modern, others solidly Victorian. The White House stood a little more than half-way up the hill, protected by a high bank which shielded all but its upper reaches from view.

Until the Victorians came to Kenley, the loose change of Empire rattling in their pockets, there were very few buildings hereabouts. Maps of the mid eighteenth century show most of the land used for agricultural purposes. Kenley's chief attraction was as a pleasure resort for Londoners seeking country air. As the local History Society has recorded:

> The earliest road from London to Brighton left the valley at the 'Royal Oak' at Purley, proceeded up Riddlesdown Road (then a lane) and crossed Riddlesdown, using part of a Roman road and rejoining the valley opposite the 'Rose and Crown'. A weekly carrier was using this road as early as 1681. In 1743 a milestone, similar to that in the grounds of Purley Hospital, was sited opposite

the pub. The old 'Rose and Crown' was a popular meeting place. On 29 April 1804, Mr Addington, a surgeon following Jenner, came here to inoculate the poor of the parish of Coulsdon against smallpox. The old Surrey Hounds met here on Saturdays and there was often a funfair, complete with shooting gallery. The coach traffic ended when steam trains ran between London and Brighton in 1841.

A lime works was opened at Kenley around 1800. The work was extremely labour-intensive and for many years the 'emphasis was on horses, men and boys to do the drudgery. Lime was sold by the yard and measured in a box which held ten bags'.

In 1869 the Caterham & Kenley Gas Company – which also used the lime from the quarries – was founded at Kenley House, close to Kenley Lane. The company was taken over by the Croydon Gas Company in 1905, 'and a new gasworks built, with great difficulty, on land which was often flooded by the Bourne'.

The White House is a large Italianate structure standing in its own grounds. An external inspection suggested a date of about 1865. The porch appeared to be of a later date, possibly added around the turn of the century. Until then the entrance may have been situated on the far side of the property, where I discovered signs of an old path. Unfortunately, these were very indistinct. (They would show up better during a heavy frost when submerged outlines become etched on the surface.)

I knew that the house had been divided into two wings about seventeen years ago. The examination furnished no significant clues except to show that the kitchens of both new divisions were more recent additions.

The general appearance of the property suggests a building date of 1865. It could not have been built in 1861 because it fails to appear on the Census return for that year. The dwelling itself first appears on a map of 1869. It must therefore have been constructed between 1861 and 1869. In the latter year it was known as Copenhagen House and occupied by one James Nichols.

James Nichols was born in 1840 at Sutton in Suffolk, a small village situated south of Woodbridge on what is now the B1083, on the edge of Sutton Common and no great distance from Hollesley Bay.

In his capacity as an East India merchant, James Nichols would have travelled widely. Strong circumstantial evidence suggests he may well have constructed the property at Kenley. Rumour suggests that he did so after falling in love with a villa of similar aspect and dimensions on the shores of Lake Como in Italy. It may be that the name reflects some business connection Nichols may have had with Denmark.

We know that James Nichols must either have inherited money or accumulated a tidy sum from business in a relatively short time, because when the Census enumerator called at Copenhagen House in 1871 Nichols was just 31 years of age. His wife, Maria, was six years older. The couple married young – when Nichols was about twenty – because their eldest child, Brigham, is shown as being ten years old in 1871. Brigham is an unusual name and it is possible that Nichols was an admirer of the American Mormon leader – and polygamist – Brigham Young, who at his death in 1877 left $2½m divided between 17 wives and 56 children.

In contrast, by 1871 James Nichols had a mere six children, produced at regular intervals of about two years. In addition to Brigham these were: Herbert, then aged 8; Ada, 6; Edith, 4; Charles, 2; and little Ella, aged 11 months.

As Charles's place of birth is given as 'Dalston, Middlesex' and Ella's as 'Coulsdon, Surrey', we know that the family moved to Kenley sometime between 1869 and 1870.

The 1871 Census reveals that James was also sheltering his unmarried sister, Rhoda, 19, a circumstance which suggests that their parents may have been dead and that at least some portion of the youthful James's wealth had been inherited.

The domestic household numbered five. With the exception of the 25-year-old gardener, Samuel Peskitt, all were female and all unmarried. There was a cook called Jane Frisbrook, 23; two housemaids, Eliza James, 24, and Patience Baker, 18; and a 'tweeny' – or between stairs maid – Sarah Harper, 14.

The history of the house over the next few years is lost to us. No rate-books survive and the County Directories are both sparse and uninformative. However, the property is briefly mentioned in the County Directory for 1878, when it is shown in the possession of a gentleman named Cecil Price. Later directories give his name as Cecil Herbert Thornton Price.

Like James Nichols before him, Cecil Herbert Thornton Price was both young and affluent. The 1881 Census gives his age as thirty. This means that when he came to the property, in about 1878, he was in his late twenties.

We know nothing concerning his early life except that he was born at Stoke Newington in 1851. The 1881 Census lists his occupation as 'Ship Insurance Broker'. He lived at Copenhagen House – which at some point he renamed The Ivies – with his wife, Ada Louisa, then 26, a native of Upton in Essex. The couple retained three servants – a cook, a parlourmaid and an under-housemaid. The latter, Emily Louisa Baker, may possibly have belonged to the same family as the Nichols's servant, Patience Baker. (It was then more usual for families to recruit domestics from the area around their new home than to carry former retainers with them.)

The County Directories continue to list Cecil Price as the occupant of The Ivies until the outbreak of the Great War in 1914 – by which time he had been in residence for at least 36 years and possibly a little longer. For the years 1915–21 the directories either fail to mention the property or show it as empty. It may be that it was during this period that some of the alterations, including the addition of the billiard room (now used as a kitchen) were probably carried out.

If so, none of the original architects' drawings have survived.

Having established from the 1881 Census that Price was born in 1851, it was clear that by 1914 (the last year in which he is shown as the occupant of The Ivies) he would have been about 63. His disappearance from the County Directories meant one of two things: either he had moved away or he had died.

There are no records which provide a satisfactory clue to house moves. I therefore decided to search the indexes of wills lodged at the Principal Registry of the Family Division in Somerset House in the hope of discovering the year of his death. I began with the last known reference in 1914. By searching forward I discovered that a will in the name of Cecil Herbert Thornton Price was probated at London in December 1920. Both the fullness of the name and the year of death suggested this was our man.

However, the Cecil Herbert Thornton Price of the indexes had been living at Woodford in Essex at the time he made his will in 1914, not in Kenley. The fact that he listed his profession as 'Wine Merchant', while the Cecil Herbert Thornton Price of the 1881 Census had given his occupation as 'Ship Insurance Broker', gave rise to further doubts. These were allayed, however, by a bequest of £100 to 'Harry West of Hermitage Cottage, Kenley Lane'.

It was clear that at some point between 1881 and the making of the will in the summer of 1914 Price had simply changed his profession. It had been a wise move financially. When he died, on 31 August 1920, aged seventy, he left an estate valued at £15,376 6s 10d, equivalent to perhaps £100,000 today.

According to the will, at the time of his death Price had two offices in the City of London. The first was at 22 Gresham House, Old Broad Street; the second at 57 Mark Lane. Both were very prestigious addresses. Kelly's street directories carried no record of the Gresham House office; but 57 Mark Lane was shown as being in the occupation of 'White & Price', wine merchants, with the telephone number AVEnue 1566. The telegraphic address 'Albariza, Fen', meant nothing to me; but its foreign flavour suggested a possible connection with the Spanish or Portuguese wine trade.

A search of the records at Companies House showed that White & Price was a well-known firm of City vintners which supplied a number of institutions, including the Mansion House (the home of the Lord Mayor) and the Travellers' Club in Pall Mall famous less for its members that those who have been black-balled from it, including Thackeray, Lord Randolph Churchill and Cecil Rhodes.

White & Price went out of business in the 1920s, soon after Price's death. Nothing material is known of Mr White, a shadowy figure who seems to have predeceased his partner.

Price appointed two executors to his will. The first was his nephew, William Harold Eve, a surveyor. The second was his solicitor ('and good friend') Edward Chapman, the senior partner in the firm of Hewitt and Chapman which had offices at 32 Nicholas Lane, City.

On reading through the will I found that it was a revised version, drawn up by Price in July 1914 . . . 'immediately after my marriage'. This came as something of a shock, furnishing as it did clear evidence that Price's first wife

CERTIFIED COPY OF AN ENTRY OF DEATH

Given at the **GENERAL REGISTER OFFICE, LONDON.**

Application Number 919524

	REGISTRATION DISTRICT			Croydon				
1910. DEATH in the Sub-district of Coulsdon in the County of Surrey								

Columns	1	2	3	4	5	6	7	8	9
No.	When and where died	Name and surname	Sex	Age	Occupation	Cause of death	Signature, description, and residence of informant	When registered	Signature of registrar
37	First May 1910 The Ivies Henley	Ada Louisa Price	Female	54 Years	Wife of Cecil Herbert Thornton Price a Wine Merchant	Fibroid Tumor of uterus Hysterectomy collapse certified by W. Blyth M.D	Ellen White Sister in Law Present at the Death Mortimer Queens Avenue Woodford Essex	Fourth May 1910	Albert Baker Deputy Registrar

CERTIFIED to be a true copy of an entry in the certified copy of a Register of Deaths in the District above mentioned.
Given at the GENERAL REGISTER OFFICE LONDON, under the Seal of the said Office, the 20th day of July 19 65.

This certificate is issued in pursuance of the Births and Deaths Registration Act 1953.
Section 34 provides that any certified copy of an entry purporting to be sealed or stamped with the seal of the General Register Office shall be received as evidence of the birth or death to which it relates without any further or other proof of the entry, and no certified copy purporting to have been given in the said Office shall be of any force or effect unless it is sealed or stamped as aforesaid.

DA 819500

CAUTION:—It is an offence to falsify a certificate or to make or knowingly use a false certificate or a copy of a false certificate intending it to be accepted as genuine to the prejudice of any person or to possess a certificate knowing it to be false without lawful authority.

CERTIFIED COPY OF AN ENTRY OF MARRIAGE

GIVEN AT THE GENERAL REGISTER OFFICE, LONDON

Application Number 919524

1914. Marriage solemnized at Christ Church in the Parish of Paddington in the County of Middlesex

Columns	1	2	3	4	5	6	7	8
No.	When Married.	Name and Surname	Age.	Condition.	Rank or Profession.	Residence at the time of Marriage.	Father's Name and Surname.	Rank or Profession of Father
244	22nd July 1914	Cecil Herbert Thornton Price	64	Widower	Wine Merchant	83 Queens Rd. W.	George William Price	Wine Merchant
		Ellen White	58	Widow	—	Mortimer, Woodford Essex	Edward Charles Curtis	Architect & Surveyor

Married in the Christ Church according to the Rites and Ceremonies of the Established Church by Licence or after — by me.

This Marriage was solemnized between us, Cecil Herbert Thornton Price / Ellen White in the Presence of us, Ellen Mohne Shutton. William Curtis Herbert Jr. Bate.

CERTIFIED to be a true copy of an entry in the certified copy of a register of Marriages in the Registration District of Paddington
Given at the GENERAL REGISTER OFFICE, LONDON, under the Seal of the said Office, the 20th day of July 19 88.

MX 193072

This certificate is issued in pursuance of section 65 of the Marriage Act 1949. Sub-section 3 of that section provides that any certified copy of an entry purporting to be sealed or stamped with the seal of the General Register Office shall be received as evidence of the marriage to which it relates without any further or other proof of the entry, and no certified copy purporting to have been given in the said Office shall be of any force or effect unless it is sealed or stamped as aforesaid.

CAUTION:—It is an offence to falsify a certificate or to make or knowingly use a false certificate or a copy of a false certificate intending it to be accepted as genuine to the prejudice of any person, or to possess a certificate knowing it to be false without lawful authority.

Form A513MX

(the Ada Louisa of the 1881 Census return) had either died or been divorced from her husband by this date. My own feeling – no more than that – was that she had departed this life shortly before her husband's remarriage. (Divorce was still relatively uncommon.)

The indexes at St Catherine's House carried only one entry for the death of an Ada Louisa Price during the relevant period – in the quarter to June 1910. From information contained in the 1881 Census it was clear that if the Ada Louisa Price of the index and Cecil's first wife were one and the same the lady would have been approximately 55 years of age at the time of her death. The index recorded an age of 56. The death was registered at Croydon, the district covering Kenley: a further indication that I was on the right track.

The certificate itself, a copy of which is reproduced overleaf, revealed that Ada Louise Price died at 'The Ivies, Henley' (sic) 1 May 1910 of a hysterectomy collapse induced by a febroid tumour of the uterus. The death was reported to the local Registrar by Ada's sister-in-law, Ellen White.

The next step was to learn something of Cecil Price's re-marriage and the identity of his new wife. The indexes at St Catherine's House showed that a Cecil H. T. Price had indeed married, during the quarter to September 1914. As Price was then living in the area, at a flat numbered 82a Queens Road, the ceremony was performed before the Paddington Registrar. The bride . . . was Ellen White.

The inference was fascinating. It is nevertheless always dangerous to jump to conclusions. The entry needed to be confirmed. To this end I carried out a counter-search. This revealed that a widow named Ellen White, the daughter of an architect and surveyor called Edward Charles Curtis, had married a Cecil H. T. Price during the same quarter. As both entries carried a similar volume and page reference it seemed highly probable – but not absolutely certain – that the two parties had married one another. It was firm enough evidence to justify investing £5 of the client's money in a copy of the certificate. In the event, it showed, as suspected, that four years after the death of his first wife, Price had married his wife's sister-in-law.

On the marriage certificate, Price's father, George William Price, is listed as 'Wine Merchant'. This suggests that the firm of White & Price had been in existence for at least two generations and possibly more.

In reporting Ada's death, Ellen White had given her address as Mortimer, Queen's Avenue, Woodford, Essex. It was from here, on 22 July, 1914, 'immediately after my marriage', that Herbert Price dated his new will, indicating that he was living by then at the home of his new wife.

Queen's Avenue still exists. A small road lying almost equidistant between Woodford Green and the M11 motorway, it is a modest thoroughfare situated at no great distance from Harts Hospital.

As the certificate shows, at the time of his re-marriage Cecil Price was 64 years old, his wife 58. Why the couple should have chosen to set up house at Mortimer rather than Kenley is a matter of conjecture. It may have been a question of economics. Common sense suggests that neither wished to start married life in a house redolent with memories of the past.

Under the terms of his new will, Price bequeathed a lump sum of £2,000 to his bride, together with 'all the houses, motor cars, horses, carriages, china, glass, books, pictures, furniture and other effects of which I may die possessed'.

Ellen was also granted the use for her lifetime of all 'my silver and jewellery'. After her death these were to pass to Price's niece, Ada Gertrude Eve, the sister of William Eve, the surveyor whom Price named as one of his executors. Both William and Ada were the children of one of Price's sisters.

Price left additional instructions that all his real estate and stockholdings should be sold, the money being used to establish a trust for the benefit first of his wife, Ellen, and then, at her death, of his niece, Ada.

Ada's brother, the surveyor William Eve, may have been left out of the will on the grounds that he was already well provided for.

★ ★ ★

As we have seen, Price's former home in Kenley stood empty from 1915 until 1920 – the same period that he lived at Woodford. This may be coincidental. There is also the possibility that Price continued to own it but was loth – perhaps for sentimental reasons – either to sell or to let it.

A local resident who knew The Ivies at this time confirms that it was allowed to fall into disrepair.

> We didn't like to pass it, not after dark. The tale was told that it had belonged to an old woman who had no money for food and died from eating string. There wasn't no truth to it, of course, but the girls always clung to your arm a bit tighter, going up that lane.

Cecil Herbert Thornton Price died 31 August 1920. By early 1921 The Ivies had come into the possession of a lady listed in the County Directories only as 'Mrs L. E. King'. Mrs King continued to be listed as the occupant until 1926, when she was replaced by Walter Robert King. Assuming that she had therefore died at around the date her name disappeared from the County Directories, and that Robert would prove to be her son, I returned to Somerset House in search of a will. The indexes for 1926 produced nothing. Those for 1927, 1928 and 1929 proved equally barren. Then, in the volume for 1930, I found an entry which read:

LAURA ELIZABETH KING

of The Ivies, Kenley Lane, Surrey (wife of Walter Robert King) died 21 November 1930 at the German Hospital, Dalston, Middlesex. Probate London 14 January 1931 to the said Walter Robert King, retired solicitor.

The White House as it stands today

This established several facts at a stroke. The first – and most interesting – was that Walter Robert King was Laura's husband, not her son. The confusion had arisen because from 1922 to 1926 the property had been listed in Laura's name solely. It was then uncommon for the directories to list a wife in preference to a husband and it occurred to me that Walter might have been living away until the latter year – either for business reasons or owing to marital discord – and that the listing in the County Directories was only changed on his return.

The entry in the index at Somerset House established the date and place of Laura's death. It did not furnish her age. The index to death certificates lodged across the way in St Catherine's House (research of this nature entails a great deal of moving about) established this as 55.

The will itself helped to flesh out the picture further. Laura left a personal estate of £1,350 – all of it to her husband, Walter. When he died, her estate was to devolve upon 'my three children, Dennis Edward Wright, Dorothy Wright and Laura Ethel Mamie Musgrave Watson provided they shall live to attain the age of twenty-one years'.

This was curious indeed. Why did none of the children bear Laura's surname? Were they adopted? Had Laura been married before? If so, the marriage could not have lasted long because all three children were clearly under the age of 21 when Laura drew up her will. She did so in her mid-fifties – another curious circumstance. Very few women of that time of life have three children all under the age of majority.

As Laura died relatively young, and soon after making her will, it seemed possible that she may not only have been the victim of a long and incurable illness but have had some intimation of her approaching end allowing her time to tidy her affairs.

The death certificate showed that she died of cancer.

A search of the registers at St Catherine's House uncovered no evidence that her husband ever remarried. Nor, although I twice carried out a thorough search of the indexes at Somerset House, could I find any reference to a will relating to him unequivocally.

What I did find were two Walter Robert Kings, either of whom might have fitted the bill.

The first died in Richmond Hospital on 19 July 1944. Both his name and the year of his death seemed plausible. The fact that he left a mere £500 was less so.

A second candidate was the Walter Robert King who died at a bungalow at Pagham Beach, Bognor Regis in 1948. He left an estate valued at £1,100, including 'a Marble Clock presented to me by Queen Alexandra at the People's Palace'.

This certainly struck the right note of grandeur. But none of the beneficiaries mentioned in the will – or indeed in the will of the other Walter Robert King – tallied with those known to have been associated with Walter and Laura King of The Ivies . . . names such as Wright and Musgrave Watson.

Consequently, our only firm knowledge of the real and authentic Walter Robert King lay in the information contained in the will of his wife. This revealed that, far from being retired, as suggested by the indexes at Somerset House, he was still a practising solicitor with offices at 142 Holborn Bars, City, at the time his wife made her will in the mid-1920s.

A long trek through Kelly's street directories uncovered a host of Kings – plumbers, upholsterers, teachers of dancing, ticket-writers, forwarding agents, linen drapers, manufacturers of desiccated soups – but no solicitors with offices in Holborn Bars. Nor was there a Walter Robert King mentioned in *Kelly's Law Directory*. I eventually ran him to earth in an obscure local directory for the Holborn area.

In addition to the office in Holborn Bars, Laura's will gave a second address for Walter – No. 66 Carlton Hill, St John's Wood. Then, as now, Carlton Hill was a residential area. It seemed unlikely that King would have used No. 66 as an office. A search of the street directories and rate-books confirmed that he occupied the house on a domestic basis – supporting the theory that he and Laura were living apart during the years 1922–26, as suggested by the County Directories for Surrey.

In fact, King occupied the house in St John's Wood for two of these years only. Where he lived for the rest of the time is not known. Nor is the nature of the couple's separation. If the problem was matrimonial it was clearly resolved satisfactorily. Had it not been, Walter would hardly have returned home or benefited under the terms of his wife's will.

Walter Robert King continued in occupation of The Ivies, Kenley Lane, until the onset of the Second World War. It then stood empty for about three years before passing to a family named Johnson of whom very little information is known.

About 1960 The Ivies was acquired from the Johnsons by a prosperous solicitor named Humphrey Bowles, senior partner in the firm of Bowles & Co., based at Epsom. Bowles lived to regret the purchase. ('I was young and foolish. Now I'm old and foolish.') The house was found to be suffering from extensive dry rot and other structural ailments.

According to the present occupant of Flat 1, Diana Dummer, Bowles purchased the property as an investment but never lived in it. Having re-christened it The White House – its third name in ninety years – he divided it up into two wings which have become separate houses in their own right. He also sold off much of the land which until this date had stretched some way up the hill.

The conversion complete, Bowles sold The White House to the 'frightfully English' Barry Mortimer, a senior public relations executive with one of the country's leading oil companies. Barry moved into Flat 2 with his wife, Fran, and their two children, Jasper and Briony. Fran proved to be 'rather arty' and 'did pottery in the cellar'.

Soon after taking over, the Mortimers disposed of the other part of the property to William F. and Diana Nita Dummer, married at this date for just four years. William Dummer was a doctor who had worked both at the Royal Northern and at Guy's Hospital in London. During his time at The White House he was employed by the pharmaceuticals group, Beechams, to research the side-effects experienced by scientists manufacturing penicillin. The fine powder which this produced was found to cause skin irritation, notably to the hands and face. Dummer devised a number of remedies, commonsense measures such as the introduction of masks and gloves and the installation of extractor fans and glass partitions.

William Dummer, 'of The White House, Kenley Lane, Kenley, Surrey', died on 22 October 1970. At the time of writing, his widow, with her daughter Lucy, continues to occupy Number 1 The White House as she has done now for the best part of thirty years.

In about 1967 Barry Mortimer's work took him to South Africa. Following a brief period of multi-occupation, Number 2 passed to Julian and Elsa Yockney. Julian's profession is unknown. Elsa was a nurse who worked the night shift at a local old people's home. She used to gaze across the valley to the yellow-lit windows of The White House, thinking of her family and wishing she were home.

The Yockneys remained in possession of Number 2 until about 1979, when they were replaced by Peter Heywood and his wife, Diane, a psychiatric social worker. According to Diana Dummer, 'Peter Heywood was an engineering journalist who used to write articles on the Forth Bridge and things like that.' He left The White House, on the break-up of his marriage. He is now working as the head of the Paris bureau of the American publishing firm, McGraw-Hill.

He was replaced at The White House by Colin Webb and his wife, Pamela, and three daughters, the present occupants of Flat 2, who first appear on the Voters' Register in 1981.

Colin Webb is the Managing Director of Pavilion Books, the publishing company which he founded in 1981 with Tim Rice and Michael Parkinson.

A Victorian Farm

Beltone Court
Near Yeovil
Somerset

When I was invited to research Beltone Court, near the small village of Hampton Marshal in Somerset, the owner informed me that the house was 'unquestionably Georgian'. An exterior inspection – an examination of the structure's symmetry, and the disposition of the doors and windows – threw this into doubt. The house had been constructed of blocks of blue lias stone quarried locally by Irish immigrant labour from the 1840s onwards.

In order to learn something about the history of the area, and about the lords of the manor of Hampton Marshal over the years, I first looked up the village in the *Victoria County History* for Somerset. This showed that in the sixteenth century the entire village had belonged to Thomas Arundell of Laherne in Cornwall, a gentleman-servant of Cardinal Wolsey. Documents in the Public Records Office at Kew affirmed that Arundell was knighted in 1533 by Henry VIII at the request of Anne Boleyn. There was an implication that he had performed some personal service for the Queen, but the exact nature of this was not recorded.

In 1619 six Hampton Marshal men were each fined sixpence (2p.) at the Hundred Court for playing bowls on a Sunday. The area was intensely Royalist and during the Civil War one landowner, Thomas Hurd, was fined the then enormous sum of £186 'for adhering to the King's party'.

Parish documents showed that an alehouse in the village was closed in

1748 because those using it were considered 'lewd and disorderly' – rural hooliganism being a problem then as now.

A scrapbook belonging to one of the older villagers contained a faded newspaper article which referred to the Miniature Rifle Club in the village in 1914. (The greatest miniature rifle expert was Lord Grey who, being a crack shot with every kind of gun, once used this little weapon to murder a perfectly innocent bumble-bee.)

Estate records lodged at the Somerset County Records Office in Taunton showed that the village was sold at auction by Sir Thomas Arundell's descendants at Garraway's Coffee-House, Change Alley, Cornhill, London in April 1801. The purchasers were a local family named Moody. A study of the memorial tablets in the church at Hampton Marshal revealed that one Aaron Moody died there in 1829, aged 79. His wife, Catherine, predeceased him by five years, dying at Hampton Marshal on 4 September 1824, aged 73.

Manorial records lodged with the County Records Office indicated that forty years later, in September 1864, the Moodys sold on to a family named Neal, who had been part of the Yeovil gentry for generations. The purchaser was William Neal, who thereafter lived at Hampton Marshal House, the local manor. As it was then quite common for gentlemen of his standing to have a London town-house as well, I decided to check his name against the alphabetical section of the London directories. This proved that William Neal owned a property in Park Crescent, a wide sweeping Nash terrace overlooking Regent's Park. He was clearly well off.

In order to learn something more about his general way of life, I searched through volumes of the *Gentleman's Magazine* in the hope of uncovering an obituary. There was the briefest possible entry. It referred to William Neal only as a 'local justice of the peace'.

I then turned to the parish registers. These indicated that William Neal fathered six sons and four daughters before his death in 1890. As he received no mention in local obituaries I decided to search out the death of his eldest son, also called William, in the hope that an obituary of him might contain some passing reference to the father. It did . . . but added nothing to what I already knew.

However, it did show that William Neal junior had been a professional soldier who rose to the rank of captain. While serving in India, he had contracted an infection, details unspecified but clearly debilitating. The hazards of the journey home, when the vessel in which he was travelling narrowly avoided shipwreck, aggravated the condition and he never fully recovered from it.

After inheriting Hampton Marshal, Captain Neal lived mostly in London. He seems not to have cared for the draughty old manor at Hampton Marshal and for most of his life it was sub-let. (As is usually the case, the names of the sub-lessees have not survived.) When Neal wished to shoot, or was forced to come to Hampton Marshal in order to attend to estate business, he rented a small cottage in his own village from his own bailiff. My impression was that his life had been one of unrelieved misery and gloom. He died without issue in 1901.

Manorial records showed that he was succeeded as lord of the manor by his brother, the Reverend John Neal. According to *Crockford's Clerical Directory,* John Neal held the curacy of several parishes. The parish registers confirmed that he died at Hampton Marshal House on Friday 17 September 1915, aged 74.

According to a report of his funeral in the local newspaper, he was buried 'in a coffin of polished oak with brass fittings'. That he had lived in some style was confirmed by the number of his servants who attended the interment. They included his bailiff, George Diment – who was then living at Beltone Court – the head estate carpenter, the head gamekeeper, the gardener and the butler. Reference to a chauffeur indicated that for the times in which he lived John Neal had been rather progressive. Not many country clergymen of his age owned cars in 1915.

Unlike his brother, William, the Reverend John Neal seems to have loved Hampton Marshal and did much to improve it. His son, John Franklin Neal, who succeeded him as lord of the manor, continued this policy. He lived at Hampton Marshal House and ran the next largest property, Beltone Court, as a farm. In good times this was done through a resident farm bailiff, as in the case of George Diment. In other times it was leased to tenants.

The Overseers' Accounts and other parish registers attested that John Franklin Neal was responsible for installing the electric lighting in the church. When he died, on 29 November 1919, he was laid to rest in the churchyard . . . close to the father whom he outlived by a mere four years.

To conclude the research into the lords of the manor of Hampton Marshal, and before turning to the history of Beltone Court itself, I walked up to Hampton Marshal House. I found it to be a handsome if rather gloomy structure which during the Second World War had been used as a hospital. In 1943 it had been converted to a school for handicapped children . . . the use that it still serves almost half a century later.

The staff, many of whom were newcomers to the village, could offer little assistance. But in talking to the kitchen and cleaning ladies, some of whom had lived in Hampton Marshal all their lives and had long memories, I learned that the children disliked walking along the Walnut Drive late at night in case they should encounter the spectral coach and horses which, it was said, still passed that way on certain nights of the year.

Laughing loudly, they repeated the rumour that there had once been a subterranean passage connecting the house with the church, but said this had long since been filled in. When asked to speculate on the purpose of this passage, they were unable to think of one, resorting to more laughter and the exchange of meaningful looks. They added that the house was said to be haunted by the ghost of a Grey Lady who stalked the third floor. Who she was, or why she had a preference for the third floor, they were unable to say. Did I believe in ghosts? I said that *appearances* were in their favour.

★   ★   ★

On horseback, Noah Mullins, bailiff to the Neals
from 1895-8, shown here with farmworkers

The Tithe map of 1839 in the County Records Office at Taunton showed the
site of Beltone Court bare of dwellings, thus confirming that the house was
early Victorian rather than late Georgian, as the owner believed. The Tithe
map denoted it only as 'Lower Ground'. At the date in question the only
occupants would have been partridge and hares.

The next line of enquiry resulted in one of those unmitigated disasters
dreaded by all researchers. All the rate-books prior to the Second World War
had been pulped in 1941 to alleviate the chronic paper shortage.

However, the Voters' Registers *had* survived, and although the earliest
were little more than a catalogue of male freeholders within the parish, they
did reveal that Beltone Court – then Beltone Farm – was constructed in 1846,
the year of its first mention.

It was occupied at this date by a 'yeoman' called William Fraser, who no
doubt held it as a tenant of the Moodys. The name of the architect had not
survived; nor, depressingly, had the deeds. Maps showed that the highway
running below the farm's bottom field was a toll-road, and thus the private
property of the Moodys. It remained a toll-road until about 1936.

When the Census enumerator called at the property in 1861, William
Fraser was still in occupation of Beltone Farm. Now aged 39, he is shown on
the returns as a 'British Subject' born somewhere in Asia in 1822. As such, he
may have been the son of an Indian Army officer. He was certainly
middle-class because he describes himself to the enumerator as 'Farmer of

400 acres employing thirteen men, six boys and three women'. Curiously, although he admits to being married, his wife does not appear on the return. She may simply have been away from home when the enumerator called; or the couple may have been estranged.

The latter theory was fuelled by the presence on the Census return of a 'visitor' – a Cornish-born 'gentlewoman' of nineteen named Elizabeth Rouse. It was highly unusual at this date for a young lady of Elizabeth's age and station to be sharing a house, unchaperoned, with a gentleman who was neither her husband nor a relative. However, it would be uncharitable to put too lewd an interpretation on this.

William Fraser retained two live-in domestics: the Wellington-born housemaid, Sarah Clay, aged 18; and an unmarried cook, Sarah Davey, 35, also Wellington-born – a circumstance which suggested that Fraser might previously have owned a house at Wellington and brought both girls with him when he transferred to Hampton Marshal. I began to speculate about Sarah Davey and to wonder whether the delicious aroma of apple pie which still 'haunts' the house from time to time might be an echo of one of her own.

★   ★   ★

At some point between 1863 and 1866, when his name disappears from the local directories, William Fraser either died or moved on. As he fails to appear in the burial register for the parish during this period, and as he would then have been only 44, the latter theory seems more likely.

By 1866 his interest in Beltone Farm had been transferred to a Cornishman named John James Bond, born at Wiveliscombe in 1832, the second year of the reign of William IV. When the Census enumerator again called at the property in 1871, Bond was entering his fortieth year. In the intervening decade the farm had expanded from four hundred to just over six hundred acres, but the number of people employed had contracted from 22 to 19, possibly as the result of increased mechanization.

Bond shared Beltone Farm with his wife, Rosina Emma, then aged 39, and his children: Mary, 11; Sarah, 10; Grace, 8; John Luff, 7; and William, 2.

Curiously, the returns list a second 'Mary Bond', aged four. As it is highly unlikely that the family would have given two of their children the same name, it may be that this second Mary was the orphaned daughter of one of Bond's close relatives – a brother, perhaps – whom James had taken in.

In the year of the 1871 Census some of the Bond children scratched their names into the glass of one of the first-floor bedroom windows. The names are still there and still decipherable. (See opposite.)

Among Bond's domestic servants in 1871 was one John Williams. A search of the churchyard revealed his grave and a headstone which recorded ('in pleasant remembrance') that he was 'for nearly twenty years a valued servant' at Beltone Farm. He died on 10 March 1886, aged 61. His wife, the former Mary Hunt, a glover, survived him by twenty years, being laid to rest beside him, on 26 March 1906, aged 68.

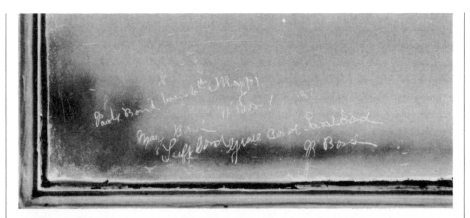

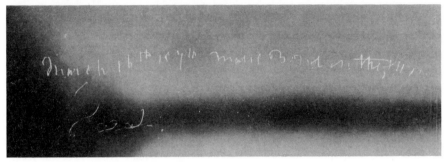

The Bond children's scratchings upon the
window pane, 1871

Infant mortality was then very high. The parish registers reveal that in August
1873 Emma Bond gave birth to her eighth child, Arthur Octavius (one
suspects that his parents had classical leanings). In September, little Arthur
Octavius was christened 'privately' at Beltone Farm, a sure sign that he was
not expected to live. He died the following February, aged six months.

When the 1881 Census was taken, neither young William Bond – who
should by all accounts have been a thriving twelve-year-old – nor his
ten-year-old brother Paul, born shortly after the previous Census, were
listed. But as a search of the burial registers failed to locate them, it is possible
that they were simply away at school.

John and Emma Bond's other children had certainly survived the decade.
They were lucky they had not been born in Hampton Marshal half a century
earlier. As the burial registers show, in the 1830s a virus passed through the
village – possible typhoid, possibly pneumonia. It killed 25 children in six
months . . . an average of one a week.

John Bond's farming interests had expanded considerably in the decade
to 1881. He now farmed 1,034 acres, more than half the total area of the
parish, and employed thirty people in the production of wheat and the rearing
of cattle. The maps showed further evidence of expansion. Slightly to the
west of the main farmhouse there was now a barn, two outhouses, and a
complex of eleven interlocked buildings arranged around a central courtyard,
used partly as farm workers' dwellings and partly for winter housing for cattle
and storage of their fodder.

This complex housed the family of one of John Bond's workers, a man called George Abel, an agricultural labourer who also doubled as the village carter. When the 1881 Census was compiled, George Abel was nearing retirement. A widower, he shared his humble dwelling with his daughter and son-in-law, George and Lydia Gulliford, both of whom were in their early thirties. The parish registers showed that George and Lydia had married in the local church on 11 January 1877. It was a double wedding, Lydia's sister, the strangely named Izett Abel, marrying Charles Parry, 'a member of the Army Hospital Corps', at the same time.

George Gulliford worked for Bond as the farm blacksmith. Although he and Elizabeth had only been married four short years when the 1881 Census was taken, they already had three children: Helen, 3; Vincent, 1; and Elizabeth, one month.

Following the fortunes of the Gullifords through the parish registers, I found that little Elizabeth died in December 1884, aged one. A fourth child, Sarah, was born to the couple later the same month. She also died – five days after her first birthday and just three days before Christmas.

Nonetheless, the Gullifords were not easily deterred. (There was little else to do on cold, dark winter evenings.) By the time Sarah died they had already produced another child, Maud, born in February 1885. A sixth, John, appeared in September 1887, and a seventh, Wilfred, in July 1889.

From an examination of the headstones in Hampton Marshal churchyard I learned that George Abel died on 29 October 1892, aged 73. His daughter, Lydia Gulliford, died in April 1902, aged 52, no doubt worn out by bearing her husband seven children in nine years. George Gulliford followed her to the grave in December 1903, aged 55, when the youngest of his children were still in their early teens. Who, one wonders, took care of them thereafter; and was the 'W. Gulliford' who fell in the First World War and is mentioned on the Roll of Honour in the church, George Gulliford's youngest? (See photograph.)

To the modern mind, George and Lydia Gulliford died young. Yet they had both attained the average life expectancy of people living in rural communities at this date. Life was hard and, despite the natural resources of the land, diets not very nutritious.

★   ★   ★

Headstone at Compton Dundon, Somerset: an example of what may be learned from inscriptions (note military insignia)

BELOW: Roll of Honour, Hampton Marshal Church

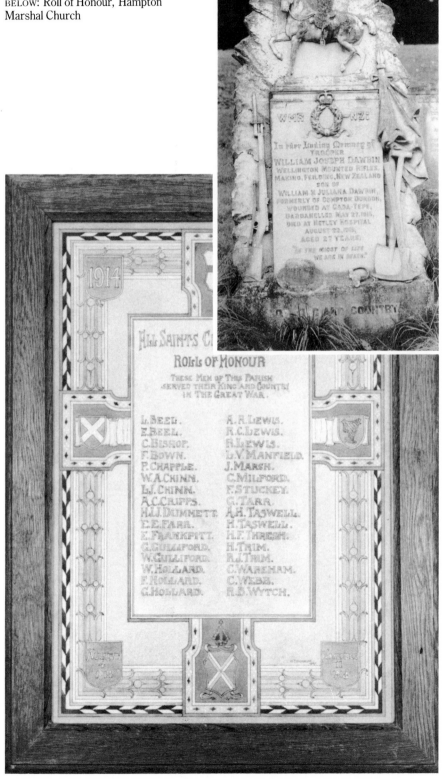

Ham stone porch at Beltone Court

John Bond, on the other hand, was living well. The Neal residence excepted, he occupied the largest house for some distance around. On 10 October 1883 his daughter, Sarah, now aged 23, married Robert Fry, a 'yeoman' of Long Sutton. Her elder sister, Mary, signed the register as a witness. The ceremony was performed by the Reverend Hansell, vicar of Hampton Marshal for sixty years from 1835 to 1895 – except for one unfortunate period of seven years when he was suspended 'for immoral behaviour with a parishioner'.

The Voters' Registers show that John Bond remained at Beltone Farm until 1890. In the same year, his son, John Luff Bond, now 24, vacated nearby Langlands Farm. It is therefore possible that father and son combined their resources and went off to farm elsewhere. That they left the village completely is apparent from the absence of any Bond names in the burial registers.

In the course of the next decade, Beltone Farm had several tenants. None can have been satisfactory, because in 1902 it was taken back into management by the Neal family, who installed their bailiff, George Diment, in the house.

Both George and his wife, Mary, were born in Devon. In 1910 George was 45 years old, 'a real old Devon bloke standing 5′9″ tall and weighing close on sixteen stone'. One parishioner who can still remember him is the son of John Neal's gamekeeper, a man called Sam Marsh.

Now 83, Marsh recalls arriving at Charlton Mackerell railway station with his father for the first time. The year was 1910, and he was then five. As their furniture, which should have preceded them, had not arrived, they lodged the first two nights at Beltone Farm. 'I've never forgotten it', Marsh told me. 'When we arrived, Mary Diment had a five-gallon pan of clotted cream on the range. She gave us some. We were Essex folk. We'd never tasted anything like it. Later, when we became more at ease, we used to burst through the kitchen door and slide across the bluestone flags.'

George and Mary Diment continued at Beltone Farm until 1919. Two years later, the Neal family sold the freehold to Humphry Lerwill. They did not, however, sell him much land, because a valuation list for 1927 in the County Records Office shows the Neals renting out four hundred acres to the Lerwills at £375 5s 0d per annum – less than a pound an acre.

Humphry Lerwill was an Overseer of the Poor and therefore something of a pillar of the community. When he died, in 1932, the running of Beltone Farm passed to his five children: Annie, Thomas, Walter, Richard and William. It seems likely that shortly before the outbreak of the Second World War they quarrelled because by 1940 the occupants of Beltone Farm had been reduced to two: Thomas and Walter, and in 1941 Beltone was put up for auction.

Even though the event took place almost fifty years ago, by asking around the village I managed to track down an elderly farmer who had been present at the sale and – more importantly from my point of view – had kept the catalogue. He didn't know why. 'I keep everything. Perhaps my Pa was going to buy it, but I shouldn't think so. Wouldn't have had the money then.'

Beltone Farm, described by the catalogue as ' a gentleman's Residence complete with two well-built cottages, farm buildings, pasture, arable and orchard lands', was to be disposed of in one lot. The purchaser was additionally required 'to take and pay for at valuation all hay, straw, and roots at market prices, and also to pay for all seeds, tillages and acts of husbandry'. 'Electricity,' it added as an afterthought, 'is available in the village adjoining.'

According to the catalogue, the basement of Beltone Farm was given over to 'extensive dry cellaring'. The ground floor accommodated an imposing entrance hall, a dining and drawing room, a large kitchen, a pantry, breakfast room, boot-house and – surprisingly – an interior dairy.

A wide staircase at the front (and a narrower one for the servants at the back) gave access to the upper floor. Here there were four major bedrooms, a dressing-room, a bathroom, a separate water closet and two maids' rooms.

The farm buildings included a 'fine Wagon House', granary boxes, a loose box, cow stalls, a piggery and four farrowing houses. One of the two

Beltone Court as it is today:
detail of stairway panelling

ABOVE: Ham stone window interior
and exterior and RIGHT: Georgian
style sash window at Beltone Court

cottages mentioned in the particulars was let on a 'tied' tenancy to an agricultural labourer employed by the Lerwills. The other was independently let to a Mr Perry at fifteen shillings (75p.) a week.

According to Sam Marsh, Beltone Farm was purchased for £8,000 by a Yeovil glover and local big-wig named Stanley Johnson, who built Johnson Park in Yeovil, donated money to the hospital, gave the town its brass band and lived in a large house on the Ilchester Road.

Johnson leased Beltone Farm to Mary's father-in-law, Robert Creed, who carried on the business of general farmer, maintaining a herd of Friesians and shorthorns, as well as a number of pigs. He was assisted by his three sons: George, who never married; Cyril, who acted as his father's chauffeur; and Ralph . . . who is still remembered in the village as an excellent left-handed shot. Cyril's wife, Mary, looked after the two thousand head of poultry.

The area opposite the walled garden was used as a dairy. The cattle were always hand-milked but, as Mary Creed recalls, despite the primitive conditions 'we never had a churn of milk returned'.

Cyril had met Mary during the war, when she was based at Yeovilton with the WRENS. One day she was out with a friend, walking on Creed land, when they were caught in a freak thunderstorm. Cyril saw them and called out: 'Quick! Under here' – holding up a tarpaulin. This was rather fitting. Mary's father was a manufacturer of tarpaulins, and this one had been made by him.

Although Cyril was fifteen years older than Mary, he was a personable man. Someone who knew him well described him as 'a large country type, fond of horses. He was very good-looking when young. He went to all the dances. All the Creeds did.' The couple married in June 1943, setting up home in one of the farm cottages, Cyril was 43, Mary 27.

During the war no fewer than eighteen bombs fell on Creed land. It seems the pilots of the Luftwaffe became convinced that Beltone Farm was Yeovilton air base. Carrying this insane idea to its illogical conclusion they mistook the farmhouse for the control tower, the outbuildings for hangars and the long drive for the runway. In an area which became known as the 'Bomb Field', but which before the war had been used to grow watercress, one missile produced a crater big enough, said Mary Creed, 'to house three double-decker buses'. Another scored a direct hit on the dairy, where George Creed was milking the cows. He escaped serious harm by ducking behind a retaining wall. Land adjacent to the 'Bomb Field' was hit by a stick of mortars – uncovering the remains of a Roman villa, the mosaics of which were removed after the war to the local museum.

Being farmers, the Creeds belonged to one of the few sections of the community which didn't go short of food. They received additional petrol coupons in order to get to and from market, as well as several allowances, including a hoeing allowance, a harvest allowance and a hay-making allowance.

Robert Creed survived the war but died in 1951, aged eighty. He had been a farmer for fifty years. His daughter-in-law recalled that he was an accomplished horseman who rode to hounds as well as point-to-point. Sam Marsh confirmed that 'old Bob Creed was the sporty type', but added rather

Original pine window shuttering with
bars in present-day drawing-room

sourly: 'He never had any money. The boys were just the same. That's why they could never afford to pay proper wages. They never didn't agree, neither.' Robert Creed chose to be buried away from Hampton Marshal, in the village of his birth. At his funeral, the church bell was tolled once for every year of his life, according to country lore.

His death had a particularly marked effect on his daughter, Edith Swanton. Edith was something of a tragic figure. She had been married only two years when her husband was killed in a hunting accident. She returned to Beltone to act as her father's housekeeper. The two were very close, but Edith had no other interests. Sam Marsh recalls: 'Never did see her out, 'cept at church.'

Edith's son, Jack was doomed like his father to meet an early end. Some years after leaving Beltone Farm for another property in the village, he announced one Boxing Day evening that he was going 'up the yard to feed the dogs'. He failed to return and was found, face down, dead in the mud. He was 46. According to one of the more ancient villagers, a man called Whitehead, 'Jack was always on the liquor – all the Creeds were. During the war I was a motorcycle despatch rider for the Home Guard. Jack was always flagging me down, looking for a lift to the pub.'

In 1953 Ralph Creed died of tuberculosis. Thereafter the two remaining sons, George and Cyril, ran Beltone Farm together. Those old enough to remember say that in its last years Beltone Farm was run much as it would have been a hundred years previously. Tom Pearce especially remembers the interior window-ledges being lined with Christmas cacti. 'They were beautiful. They made a real impression on me.'

The house boasted no fewer than three grandfather clocks and the parlour was filled with stuffed birds, each enclosed in an ovular glass case. At night, the house was lit by 'twenty-one oil lamps'. There were large quantities of Victorian silver and glass, two or three superb but dilapidated chaise-longues, and four half-tester four-poster beds.

The cellar, which contained an open well and a vast old cider-press, was used for the storage of home-made cider. Great hams hung from the ceiling, together with sirloins of beef and quarters of lamb. Here the bacon was salted, and here, every Easter, a young calf was prepared for the table.

For all this, life at Beltone Farm was essentially primitive. The house had only one bathroom, and that inadequate. The telephone was installed in 1947, but it was left to the present owner to install electricity – in 1965. The fireplaces, while impressive to look at, gave off precious little heat. It was a desperately raw house in winter.

For many years, after Robert Creed became infirm, what is now a very elegant dining-room served as his bedroom. The family more or less lived in what is now a small study, 'taking their meals before the fire and looking out through the window'. The present studio and work area was then the dairy, where muddy and pungent cattle were tethered, partly in and partly out of the house.

The lounge – called the parlour by the Creeds – housed an immense oak table, seating eighteen. But the room was only occasionally used . . . for parties and Christmas lunch. The chairs which complemented this were ladder-backed, the seats stuffed with horsehair. This was a matter of indifference to the adults, who wore trousers or long thick skirts, but according to Mary Creed the children found it tickled the backs of their thighs in a very unpleasant manner.

The parlour also housed a Jacobean bureau and an old school desk, disfigured by a heavy ink-stain etched into its top. Mary Creed was fond of telling visitors that this had been done by Nelson – and so it had . . . but not the admiral, one of his descendants.

The kitchen contained the usual farmhouse knick-knacks: cream jugs commemorating Queen Victoria's Golden and Diamond Jubilees of 1887 and 1897; coronation mugs and plates recording the accessions of Edward VII and George V; willow-pattern china (some of it very good); silver carving sets;

Original early-Victorian fireplace

knives and forks with yellowing bone handles so ancient that they could never be washed in hot water in case the glue should come unstuck.

The bedrooms had no running water. On rising in the morning the occupants performed their ablutions with the aid of a water-jug and bowl. In winter it was sometimes necessary to break the thin film of ice first.

* * *

Although they worked Beltone for many years, for most of this time the Creeds were never more than tenants. Stanley Johnson, who had bought the property at the auction in 1941, remained their landlord.

In 1959 they learned – from Johnson's chauffeur – that the Yeovil big-wig was proposing to sell the farm over their heads. Johnson's housekeeper, who had a soft spot for the family, eventually persuaded her employer to give the Creeds first refusal. They purchased the house and two hundred acres of farmland for £14,000. The rest of the farmland was disposed of by Johnson to other local farmers.

Once the danger had passed, life reverted to normal. George and Cyril continued to hunt, ride and shoot – 'going after pheasants, duck or partridge, in fact anything for the pot'. The beginning of the end dawned when Cyril developed cataracts – which meant he could no longer drive – as well as a serious throat problem.

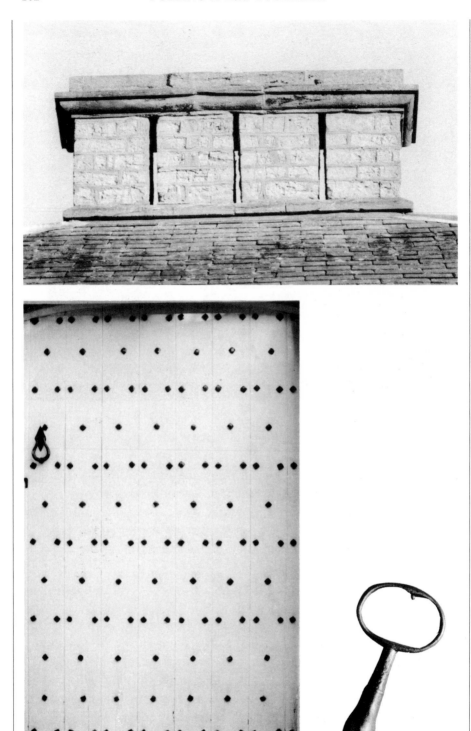

Various clues to Beltone Court's history

At this time Cyril and Mary were still living in the cottage they had first moved into at the time of their marriage in 1943 – the 'big house' being reserved for George, his sister Edith Swanton and Edith's son, Jack. They had never modernised the place – possibly through lack of money – and conditions were primitive. The toilet was an *Elsan*, the cause of much trouble and inconvenience. When Cyril's young nephew returned from a stay at the cottage and was asked to compose a school essay on 'What I did in the Holidays', he wrote: 'Uncle Cyril took the toilet for a walk.'

With Cyril incapacitated, the day-to-day running of the farm devolved upon George, Jack and Edith. But none of them were getting any younger and it rapidly became too much. The Creed good looks had faded, and the days when they had attended 'all the dances' were now just a memory. Mole hills began to appear. In time they became so numerous and large that not even the great wheels of the tractor could surmount them. Events – and progress – had overtaken the Creeds. Their day had passed. In 1965 they decided to sell.

In the words of Mary Creed, 'the sale was a mockery.' A buyers' ring operated, and many items were knocked down at less than their true worth. Two Jacobean dressers went for next to nothing. A beautiful settle, almost certainly as old as the house itself, was ripped out in two parts and burned as so much firewood. The stuffed birds were also burned, their glass cases having first been smashed to pieces with pick-axes. The four-posters swayed off down the drive, precariously roped over, in a procession of lorries and horse-drawn carts.

Some items, which collectors and museums would now covet, were destroyed in an orgy of gleeful and mindless vandalism. The 'dear old thresher', which had given years of faithful service, was mercilessly dragged from the Wagon House and set on fire. A similar fate befell a haywain, a pretty painted little gig, a governess's cart, and a defenceless button-backed landau with its stuffing hanging out. Also burnt was the once brightly-painted and brass-railed wagon which Robert Creed had used to drive down into Hampton Marshal each day during the war, drawn by his faithful pony, Kitty, for his lunchtime drink.

Tom Pearce recalls a band of gypsies purchasing 'a load of scrap metal for a pound'. Among this was 'an old sword'. Pearce admits: 'It didn't look much. Still I offered 'em ten shillings (fifty pence) for it. I had 'un cleaned. Turned out to be a Dragoon's sword, very old. I put 'un in Wallace's sale an' 'un fetched fifty quid.' He added: 'I also got some rabbit gin-traps cheap.'

Some things did attract a fair price, notably the cattle and the magnificent prize bull, Marmaduke. Two meat-dishes which the Creeds thought junk fetched £100 and £50 respectively. A chair, which when turned upside down converted into a pair of library steps, was also the subject of unexpectedly fierce bidding.

The sale over, the Creeds moved out to a house in the village, where they kept a donkey and a couple of sheep – 'to remind themselves they had once been farmers'.

It now only remained to sell the house and farmland. It was eventually purchased by a local landowner, who kept the land and sold the house to its present owner. Denuded of all but six acres of garden land, it was modernized, gentrified and renamed Belstone Court.

In the twenty years since then it has been used as a family home. It has a pleasant, relaxed atmosphere which tends to cause strangers to fall asleep within half an hour of entering it. There are few reminders of the days when it stood at the hub of a thousand-acre farming operation . . . merely a few faded initials etched in the panes of one of the bedroom windows.

A House in Mayfair

No. 16 Charles Street
London W1

In the spring of 1988 I was approached by Suzie Arthur, the American head of the film-makers, Locomotive Productions, with a request to research the history of No. 16 Charles Street, Mayfair. The property had been used for location shots for a film with which she had been associated. Having become intrigued by the house, she found herself wanting to know more about its history.

The commission struck a responsive chord. I live in London and frequently pass down Charles Street. I had for some time been speculating about No. 16 myself. There were no 'For Sale' boards outside, but it was clearly empty and semi-derelict. I wondered who might have lived there; and what they would feel if they could see it now. I felt sorry for the house.

★   ★   ★

Much of the historical information on Charles Street is lodged with the local history and archives department of Westminster City Libraries, located in Buckingham Palace Road.

John Rocque's map of 1746 showed that the street covered the route of an ancient bridle path, a tributary of what is now Berkeley Square. At this date, Charles Street was shown only in outline, none of the dwellings being built. The card in the rate-book index confirmed that the street was first rated in the early years of the next decade.

The garden – unusual in a London club

It was not possible to establish the fact for certain, but the balance of probabilities suggested that the builder was a carpenter turned speculative developer named John Phillips, who in December 1750 took much of the land hereabouts on lease from Lord Berkeley, the ground landlord. Phillips had his workshop in a timbered house at the corner of Charles and Waverton Streets. It was typical of the kind still occasionally seen in old seaside towns and was extant as late as 1927.

By searching the cards of the Illustrations Index I found several pictorial references. One of these, a line drawing from the *Illustrated London News*, showed that Phillips' workshops were disposed on various floors. They were

The dining-room of the Guards' Club

connected by a series of almost vertical ladder-like stairs, with ropes for handrails.

Before studying the house itself I decided to learn something about the area. Gillian Bebbington's *London Street Names* records that Charles Street was dedicated to the memory of a relative of the ground landlord, Charles Berkeley, Earl of Falmouth, who lost his life fighting against the Dutch at the naval battle off Southwold Bay in 1665.

Scouring the indexes of a number of topographical works on Mayfair I discovered several references to Charles Falmouth. The most bizarre recounted that at the height of the action his head was carried away by a cannon ball. This caused a callous fellow officer to bray: 'Ah! The first and last proof that Falmouth had brains.'

Mayfair has always been a haunt of the rich and famous. Because I always give a general account of the history of an area before moving on to a study of a specific property, and because I found Charles Street especially rich in associations, I decided to mention half a dozen of its luminaries in some detail in my report.

Perhaps the most eminent was the Duke of Clarence, afterwards William IV, who lived at No. 20. His entry in the *Dictionary of National Biography* provided a great deal of basic information. To supplement this with a sprinkling of anecdote, I went to the reading room of the British Museum (officially known as the British Library) and ordered up as many works on him as I could find. There were more than I could possibly read. I therefore flicked through the indexes looking for references to unusual characteristics or behaviour. I found a great many. William IV was one of the greatest eccentrics ever to mount the throne of England.

A typically libidinous Hanoverian, William produced ten children in fifteen years by the popular Irish actress, Dorothea Jordan. When he endeavoured to reduce her housekeeping, Mrs Jordan responded by handing him a copy of the statutory regulation then attached to all play-bills: 'No money refunded after the rising of the curtain.'

William did not become king until the death of his brother, George IV, in 1830. For much of his life he therefore enjoyed a great deal of freedom and privacy. He was very fond of walking and was often to be seen striding down Charles Street, his pineapple-shaped head bobbing up and down in a very curious manner. He had the habit of thinking aloud and when a prayer was offered for rain, he was heard to remark, rather gloomily: 'No good when the wind's in the south-east.'

He was also cursed with the Hanoverian attachment to triptology – the compulsive habit of saying everything three times. When the preacher announced, 'Let us pray,' the Duke responded, 'By all means, by all means, by all means.' When the same cleric observed that we come naked into the world and can take nothing from it, the Duke muttered, very audibly: 'True, true, true. Too many demands on us for that.'

Old and New London states that the Duke's home in Charles Street was later occupied by the fifth Earl of Rosebery, the Liberal politician who became prime minister in 1894. The Dictionary of National Biography reveals that he was a keen racing man and had three Derby winners. On looking him up in various dictionaries of quotation, I found that Rosebery is generally credited with being the first man to describe the British Empire as 'a Commonwealth of Nations' – and his countrymen as 'a nation of amateurs'.

The great Regency dandy, George (Beau) Brummell was another Charles Street resident. He once applied to his neighbour, Scrope Davies, for a 'loan', which he intended to use to flee to France in order to escape his creditors. He sent over a note by his valet, requesting to borrow '£500 for a few days. The funds are shut for the dividends or I should not have made this request.' The wily Scrope Davies, perhaps sensing the imminence of disaster, replied: 'My Dear Brummell; All my money is locked up in the funds.'

This occasion apart, Scrope Davies was not a hard-hearted man. Having relieved a young fool of his entire inheritance at the card-table, he cheerfully returned it, exacting only a promise that the youth would foreswear gambling for the future.

For many years, No. 33 Charles Street was the home of Lady Margaret Fitzgerald. She burned to death here in 1815, along with her daughter. She went to the grave without ever having learned the truth surrounding the death of her son – the infamous 'Fighting' Fitzgerald – who had been hanged at Tyburn 30 years earlier as a common criminal. The facts had been scrupulously concealed from her by her family.

As records suggest 'Fighting' Fitzgerald may have lived for a time with his mother, his story has some relevance. I was able to piece it together from contemporary newspaper reports, various works on Georgian London, and an amusing account contained in Tom Girtin's *The Abominable Clubman*.

An aristocratic psychopath, 'Fighting' Fitzgerald was a familiar sight around Mayfair and St James's. If he had lived today he would probably have been a football hooligan. He drank copious draughts of his own blood in the belief that it would prolong his life by a thousand years; kidnapped his own brother; and imprisoned his father in a cave with a wild bear.

On another occasion, while weighing himself in the condiment scales at the Widow Berry's shop in St James's Street (a shop little changed and now occupied by the wine merchants, Berry Bros & Rudd) he was interrupted by an acquaintance who, sticking his head round the door, remarked: 'Fee, fie, foe fum, I smell the blood of an Irishman.' Leaping from the scales – which can still be seen in the shop – Fitzgerald snarled: 'Then I'll be damned if you ever smell the blood of another', drew his sword and promptly cut off the man's nose.

Like most outcasts, Fitzgerald craved respectability. To this end he proposed himself for membership of one of the most august gentlemen's clubs in London. To ensure that he was voted in, he arrived a little before the time appointed for the election and positioned himself on a chair in the hall, resting a large wooden club across his broad knees.

Although each committee member had to pass him on arrival, 'each without exception blackballed him in the vote'.

When the news was conveyed to the hall, Fitzgerald calmly insisted that there must have been 'some mistake' and urged the members to vote again. They did – with the same result.

At this, Fitzgerald mounted the stairs two at a time, burst into the committee room and, thrusting his big red face into that of each of the committee members in turn, enquired: 'Was it you who blackballed me?' Naturally, all denied it. 'Why then,' said he, 'I am got in' – and ordered up several bottles of the club's best port to celebrate the fact.

Determined to prevent him re-entering the club, the committee hired six prize-fighters to bar the door. Strangely, 'Fighting' Fitzgerald never returned. It seems that to have 'got in' was enough.

Exterior of No. 16 Charles Street, 1987

In 1988 very little has changed, due to
lengthy territorial disputes

Fitzgerald's desperate character eventually led him to kill a man. For this he was sentenced to hang at Tyburn. His 'damned thick Irish neck' broke the rope and he plummeted into the crowd, landing on his feet and saying with a grin: 'I see I am amongst you once again.'

He was not so lucky a second time.

By searching family pedigrees I came to the conclusion that at least some of Fitzgerald's madness may have been inherited. His mother's brother, the Bishop of Derry, appears to have had no wits at all. On a visit to Italy he insisted on peering into an erupting volcano, sustaining injuries which soon after proved fatal. In order to conceal from a superstitious crew that he had a corpse on board, the captain of the vessel charged with returning the Bishop's corpse to England packed it in a crate which he labelled 'Antique Statue'.

'Fighting' Fitzgerald's home in Charles Street later became the London residence of the witty Regency cleric, Sydney Smith, who in November 1835 wrote to a friend: 'I have bought a house in Charles Street, lease for fourteen years, for £1400 and £10 per annum ground rent.' He called the house 'The Hole', adding: 'The lawyers discovered some flaw in the title about the time of the Norman Conquest. But thinking the parties must have disappeared in the quarrels of York and Lancaster I waived the objection.'

In January 1875, having spent Christmas with the Marlboroughs at Blenheim, Lord and Lady Randolph Churchill moved into No. 48 Charles Street with their two-month-old son, Winston. His mother, the eccentric Lady Randolph – formerly the American heiress, Jenny Jerome – shocked her neighbours by sporting the only tattoo in polite society – a butterfly on her left wrist.

However, as I found on checking through various guides to literary London, Lady Randolph was not the most eccentric resident of Charles Street. That honour was reserved for Edward Bulwer, better known in later life as Sir Edward Bulwer-Lytton, the highly successful Victorian novelist. In 1831, as a young man, he occupied rooms at No. 2, an upper-class rooming house run by a couple named Urquhart.

Lytton, like Brummell before him, was then a fanatical dandy who spent hours in front of a mirror adjusting a crease or a strand of hair. Disraeli, something of a dandy himself in youth, made reference to this when speaking of Charles Greville, whom he called 'the most conceited person with whom I have ever been brought in contact – although I have read *Cicero* and known Bulwer-Lytton.'

According to the *Oxford Book of Literary Anecdote*, this same conceit led Bulwer-Lytton to believe he was omnipotent. One morning at Knebworth, his country seat in Hertfordshire, some guests were eating breakfast when, to their utter astonishment, Lord Lytton entered the room, unkempt and wearing a dressing-gown. Without acknowledging their presence, he shambled round the table, peering intently into each face in turn. His wife muttered, 'Take no notice. He thinks he is invisible.'

The editor of the first volume of Augustus Hare's quirky biography, *In My Solitary Life*, says that Lady Bulwer-Lytton had been a Miss Rosina

Wheeler. Lytton had married her against his mother's wishes. After nine years they were legally separated, and thereafter Lady Lytton devoted herself to making various public attacks on her husband, enshrining him as the villain of her novel, *Cheveley*, and on one occasion denouncing him from an election platform.

In fact, Lady Lytton was making attacks on her husband well before their separation. She once remarked: 'He ought to have gone to the colonies long ago, and at the Queen's expense.' When Wilkie Collins published *The Woman in White*, she wrote to congratulate him, but added:

> You really do not know a villain. Your Count Fosco is a very poor one and when you next want a character of that description I trust you will not disdain to come to me. I know a villain and have one in my eye this very moment that would far eclipse anything that I have read of in books. Don't think that I am drawing upon my imagination. This man is alive and constantly under my gaze. IN FACT HE IS MY OWN HUSBAND.

If Bulwer-Lytton was unhappy in his choice of wife, he was much consoled by his children. They loved him dearly and were always thinking up ways to please him. One evening they put on a costume drama depicting the return of a crusader from the Holy Land. After the warrior had been recounting his exploits for some time, his 'wife' suddenly produced a string of 'babies' – her dolls – and uttered the immortal remark: 'I too, my lord, have not been idle.'

The novels of Bulwer-Lytton belonged to what was known as 'the Silver-Fork School'. But their author's own pedigree was suspect. As Augustus Hare put it: 'I wish that one did not know that the real name of the Lyttons is Wigett!'

How long Lord Lytton remained in Charles Street is uncertain. Nor do we know whether it was here, or at one of his ten other Mayfair addresses, that he fitted up his chambers to resemble a Roman brothel.

A keen spiritualist who made strenuous efforts to 'get in touch' with his dead daughter, he eventually became disgusted by the vulgarity of the medium. By way of illustration he used to recount a conversation he had once heard at a seance between a lady and her departed husband:

'Are you,' asked the lady, 'quite 'appy, dear – as 'appy as when you was with me?'

'Oh, far, far 'appier.'

'Then indeed you must be in 'eaven,' sighed the lady.

'No,' returned the gentleman. 'I'm in 'ell.'

Bulwer-Lytton died in January 1873. His body had hardly been laid to rest in Westminster Abbey when a movement was started to rename Charles Street 'Lytton Street' in his honour. A successful revolt against this idea was instigated by the great political hostess, Lady Dorothy Neville, a friend of Disraeli, who lived in Charles Street for most of her life.

★　★　★

The stairway, restored to something of its
former glory for the making of a film in the 1980s

It would be tiresome in recounting the history of No. 16 Charles Street to list
all the sources consulted in detail. Many will be obvious. A good number of the
remainder are those cited in previous chapters. However, I cannot proceed
without first acknowledging the help afforded me by the *Survey of London*,
which provided much invaluable information regarding the early occupants.

No. 16 Charles Street was constructed as a town-house for Francis
Willoughby, second Baron Middleton (1692–1758). When it was completed –
in 1753 – the area was still quite rural. Park Lane was a lonely mud-encrusted
track; sportsmen hunted snipe along the hedgerows; and Berkeley Square
was bordered to the south by what the Vestry Minutes refer to as an open
'common sewer'.

Educated at Eton (1707–8), Lord Willoughby served as Tory member of
parliament for Nottinghamshire, the county in which many of his ancestors had

Similarly restored is the elegant reception
room at No. 16

resided. He lived at No. 16 with his wife Mary, the daughter of a Middle
Temple barrister named Thomas Edwards.

Five years after his arrival at Charles Street, Middleton died, while on a
visit to Bath. He was 65. His widow then moved away and the house was sold
to a family named Craven. With the exception of the occasional sub-letting,
few details of which have survived, they occupied it for 126 years – until 1884.

The first Craven to live at No. 16 on a permanent basis was William
Craven, born in nearby Hill Street in September 1770. In 1793 he purchased a
Lieutenant-Colonelcy in the 84th Foot. According to the *Complete Peerage*, he
is said 'to have given a larger sum for this than was ever paid before'.

In 1801 William was created Viscount Uffington and Earl of Craven. Five
years later, at his house in Charles Street, he married Louisa Brunton, who
was 'a great beauty and an actress at Covent Garden'.

The first Earl Craven was a crony and drinking companion of the Prince Regent (afterwards George IV), and in 1815, the year of the battle of Waterloo, entertained his fellow roustabout at his country seat, Combe Abbey, near Coventry.

By May 1825 the Earl of Craven had risen to the rank of General. An implacable opponent of all reform, especially Catholic emancipation, he was an able if stern Recorder of Coventry.

His private life, however, was less than spotless; and he is best remembered today for his liaison with the beautiful demi-rep, Harriette Wilson, who became his mistress when she was just fifteen. According to her *Memoirs*, he entertained her by drawing pictures of cocoa trees and by wearing in bed 'an ugly cotton nightcap'. Harriette soon left him for the handsome Lord Ponsonby, muttering: 'I shall hate cocoa as long as I live.'

Among Harriette's other amours was the Duke of Wellington. When her beauty faded she threatened to publish her memoirs in the hope of extracting money from those of her former lovers who would wish to be kept out of them. But when she approached the Iron Duke with this proposition he uttered the legendary remark: 'Publish and be damned!' She did – but the book did him no lasting harm.

The second Earl of Craven was born in 1809. Like his father before him, he became Recorder of Coventry; and – again like his father – died relatively young. The third Earl, George Grimston Craven, was born at 16 Charles Street on 16 March 1841. In politics a Liberal, and a sometime Lord Lieutenant of Berkshire, he became such a valued customer of the tobacconists, Carreras, that they named a brand of cigarette after him – 'Craven A'.

When, after a long illness, the third Earl died in his forty-third year, a rumour began to circulate that all the Cravens were destined to predecease their mothers – allegedly the result of a curse placed on the family by a maid-servant who is said to have given birth to a stillborn son fathered by a Craven heir.

The Curse of the Cravens has not proved consistently fatal, but sufficient Earls have met premature ends to ensure that it is taken seriously. The first Earl died of gout, at the age of 54, and the second Earl of paralysis, at 57. His eldest son and heir, Viscount Uffington, died at 16 Charles Street in April 1865, aged 26. As we have seen, his brother, the third Earl, was a chronic invalid who died in his early forties.

In 1921, the fourth Earl drowned at Cowes, aged 53, when he fell overboard from his yacht in full evening dress. His cries for help went unheeded because they were not thought to have 'emanated from anyone of importance'.

In the autumn of 1923, the fifth Earl – known as One-Leg Craven – created a sensation by eloping with the Countess Cathcart. The couple were reported to be travelling with 36 packing cases filled with antiques which the Earl had removed from Combe Abbey. He died in 1932 aged 35.

The sixth Earl lived long; but in 1983 the seventh Earl shot himself at the age of 26. According to newspaper reports, he left three-quarters of a million pounds to his two-year-old illegitimate son, Tommy – whose mother, Anne Nicholson, was living in a council flat at Helensburgh near Glasgow, supporting herself and her son on £25 a week social security.

At that date, the present Earl was a trainee chef at Eastbourne College. He said that he was 'not at all worried by the curse', adding: 'If there is one, I certainly intend to prove it wrong.'

★   ★   ★

On the advice of his doctors, the third Earl Craven spent little time at No. 16, and when the Census enumerator called at the property in 1881 he found the house sub-let to George Watson Milles, first Earl Sondes of Lees Court.

Lord Sondes, who was then 57, shared the house with his wife, Charlotte, forty and their three daughters, aged respectively twenty, seventeen and fifteen. They are identified on the Census returns only as 'Lady M', 'Lady L' and 'Lady E'.

Lord Sondes' eldest son, George, afterwards the second Earl, is not shown on the return as he was then living elsewhere. He died in 1909 of wounds received while serving with the Imperial Yeomanry in the Boer War. He was thus the first of two occupants of No. 16 who, quite independently, were to suffer similar fates. (The other was Herbert Magniac, of whom more later.)

The Sondes household, which consisted of five, was served by a staff of fourteen. There was a butler, James Edis, 40; a governess for the girls, Edith Pontgrain, 35, who after the fashion of the day may have been French; a cook named Mrs Aubrey, 30; and three ladies' maids. These were the senior servants. There were also two footmen, George Barnwell and Albert Townsend, both aged 21; two housemaids; a schoolroom-maid; and a 'hall man', John Hooper, 51. With the exception of Hooper, Edis and Mrs Aubrey, none of the staff was married.

★   ★   ★

When the third Earl of Craven died in 1883, the Craven family's tenure of No. 16 came to an end. The house then stood empty for the best part of two years before being taken by Charles Magniac, member of parliament for Bedford, who no doubt used it as his London base during the parliamentary term. He lived here with his wife, Augusta, a daughter of Lord Castletown, and their son, Herbert, then aged 29.

Herbert Magniac was to achieve considerable distinction as a soldier. In fact he was an old-fashioned hero who could have come straight from the pages of *Boys Own*.

At the outbreak of the Boer War in 1899 he was one of the first to volunteer for service with the Imperial Yeomanry. Joining as a subaltern, he eventually became second in command of his regiment. He possessed a form of cool courage that bordered on the foolhardy. Here is an extract from his obituary in *The Times*:

He distinguished himself on several occasions, notably at the attack on Modderfontein when, with a handful of Yeomanry, he defended a position on the flanks for nearly twenty-four hours, by which time the relieving force should have arrived. In the course of this fight all his men but one were killed or wounded, and he himself was hit three times. Summoned to surrender, he stoutly refused, although he had only two cartridges left, and jumping up he shot the Boer leader dead at fifteen yards and the Boers retired. He received several fresh wounds in the attack and was returned suffering from seventeen gunshot wounds.

For this quite remarkable feat of bravery, Magniac received one of the first awards of the Distinguished Service Order. However, although 'he made a miraculous recovery from his wounds and from pneumonia and enteric fever, which followed from exposure . . .', Major Magniac was never the same man again. In 1909 the wounds received in South Africa indirectly brought about his death. On 24 March he passed away at his chambers in the Albany, at the age of 43. He thus became the fifth some-time occupant of 16 Charles Street to die prematurely.

★   ★   ★

Charles Magniac, Herbert's father, shared 16 Charles Street with his stepsons, Vesey and Douglas Dawson, whose father, Lieutenant-Colonel the Hon. T. Vesey Dawson, had been killed in the Crimea at the battle of Inkerman when they were eighteen months and six months old respectively. Both brothers joined the Coldstream Guards and both served in the Nile Expedition of 1884–5.

In 1900 Vesey Dawson was appointed to the command of the Irish Guards. He was made C.V.O. in 1902 and retired from the army in 1914 with the rank of Major-General. He died, aged 76, on 17 January 1930 at Remenham Place, Henley-on-Thames, the residence of his brother.

Brigadier-General Sir Douglas Dawson was educated at Eton where he was in Mr Oscar Browning's house. He was a keen cricketer and 'having developed a slow over-hand action, distinguished himself by taking nine wickets in three overs in a house match.'

In 1872 he joined the army. He also acquired an exceptional knowledge of foreign languages. In 1883 he was selected for special service in Egypt under Sir Garnet Wolseley; and took part in the battle for Kassassin, where his horse was shot under him. He saw further action during the Sudan Expedition of 1884 as a member of that most unlikely of military groupings, the Guards' Camel Corps.

In 1890 Dawson was appointed military attaché to Vienna. Five years later, he was transferred to Paris. In 1927 he published an entertaining volume of reminiscences, *A Soldier Diplomat*, which gives a vivid picture of his life and times. He was on intimate terms with the Austrian Emperor, Francis Joseph, and played an important mediating role in the Dreyfus Case.

In 1903 he received the first of several Court appointments which were to occupy the next twenty years of his life. During this time he was successively Master of the Ceremonies to Edward VII; and Secretary to the Order of the Garter and to the Order of Merit. In 1919 he was appointed an Extra Equerry to George V.

Sadly, his last years were clouded by financial hardship. Having, in his own words, 'never professed to be a judge of finance or investments', he foolishly agreed to join the board of City Equitable. When that company failed, his health broke down. He died on 20 January 1933, aged 77, having survived his brother by three years.

★ ★ ★

In the last years of the Victorian era 16 Charles Street passed from the Magniac family to the Rt Hon. William McEwan MP, the founder of the brewery company of the same name which still produces McEwan's lager. McEwan lived at 16 Charles Street until his death in 1913 at the age of 85.

He bequeathed the bulk of his fortune, valued at over £1½m, to his stepdaughter, Margaret Greville. He also left her his country seat, Polesden Lacey, near Dorking – and 16 Charles Street.

Margaret's first act on taking possession of No. 16 was to commission the architects Charles Mewes (a Frenchman from Alsace) and his partner, Arthur J. Davis, both schooled in the *Beaux-Arts* movement, to redesign and extend the rear of the property, and to decorate the walls of the ballroom in eighteen carat gold-leaf.

Mewes & Davis was an immensely fashionable and successful firm which completed a number of such commissions during this period, including the Ritz Hotel in Piccadilly – London's first steel-framed building – and 88 Brook Street, for Henry Coventry.

★ ★ ★

By the time she came to No. 16, Maggie Greville was a widow. Her husband, Captain the Hon. Ronald Greville, 1st Life Guards, had been the elder son of the second Lord Greville and a close friend of Edward VII. He eventually left the army for politics, sitting as Unionist member for East Bradford. Although married for seventeen years, the Grevilles had no children. In April 1908 Ronald Greville became the sixth person associated with the property to die prematurely when, at the age of 45, he expired following an operation for cancer of the throat.

The Hon. Mrs Ronnie Greville occupied 16 Charles Street for thirty years up to her death in September 1942. During this time she became one of the greatest society hostesses London has ever known. *The Times* wrote at the time of her death: 'She was a lady of strong character and practical ability, and it pleased her to use the great wealth which she inherited for the purpose of a wide but discriminating hospitality.'

During her tenure everyone of note came to No. 16 – Churchill's right-hand-man, Brendan Bracken, the Mountbattens, the Kents, the Yorks. The King of Greece was embarrassed by the rich food because it made him think of his starving compatriots. The King and Queen of Spain were not.

Mrs Greville was on equally intimate terms with British royalty, and the Yorks continued to visit No. 16 after succeeding to the throne as George VI and Queen Elizabeth. Mrs Greville bequeathed most of her fabulous jewellery to the Queen, now the Queen Mother.

The Hon. Mrs Ronnie Greville was well known in the worlds of business and politics alike. Her friendships were many and diverse. Not all her hospitality, however, was as 'discriminating' as her *Times* obituarist – even writing with the benefit of hindsight – seems to have believed. As Carol Kennedy attests in *Mayfair: A Social History*:

> Some hostesses were openly pro-Nazi, Maggie Greville among them. Harold Nicolson loathed the atmosphere at her dinner parties at 16 Charles Street, where Ribbentrop and the Italian Ambassador, Count Grandi, flattered and were fawned upon by sycophantic socialites. He expressed hope in his diary for 1939 that Berlin and Rome would realise that British will-power was concentrated 'not in Mayfair or Cliveden (the Astor estate by the Thames), but in the provinces. The harm which these silly, selfish hostesses do is really immense. They convey to foreign envoys the impression that policy is decided in their own drawing-rooms . . . these people have a subversive influence.'

Small, round and fat – looking in her god-daughter's words like 'a small Chinese idol' – Mrs Greville was possibly:

> . . . the biggest snob in Mayfair and was noted for that memorable piece of one-up-man-ship: 'One uses up SO many red carpets in a season.' Beverley Nichols, who recorded the remark, said: 'there were enchanted nights in the Twenties when the people around Grosvenor Square were giving so many grand parties that the pavements were as bright as a sunset.' Indeed, a king or other crowned head was frequently in attendance at Maggie Greville's dinners where, out of sixty or so guests, fifty might be titled.

★　★　★

The dining-room of the club
with its fine ornamentation.

On 13 December 1922 – the year Mrs Greville was made a Dame of the Order of the British Empire – the Prince of Wales (afterwards Edward VIII) attended a dance at 16 Charles Street. Also present were Lord and Lady Louis Mountbatten, recently returned from a long honeymoon in California where Lord Louis had appeared in a short film with Charlie Chaplin.

Mrs Greville's name was now seldom out of the newspapers. In 1923 – the year 'One-Leg Craven' shocked Society by eloping with the Countess Cathcart – it featured again when she loaned Polesden Lacey to the newly-wed Duke and Duchess of York for their honeymoon.

In May 1924, according to Andrew Barrow, the author of *Gossip: 1920–1970*,

> . . . the Duke of Westminster suddenly withdrew permission for Grosvenor House, his vast home in Park Lane, to be used for a ball in aid of the Italian Hospital. Society hostess, Mrs Ronnie Greville, immediately offered the use of 16 Charles Street. On the night of the dance, the house was so packed that the King and Queen of Italy had to sit waiting in their car while footmen cleared a pathway through the crowds and upstairs to the ballroom.

On 12 July 1927 King Faud of Egypt dined at No. 16; and on 29 November 1932 Mrs Greville attended the marriage of Churchill's daughter, Diana, at St Margaret's, Westminster.

By now, however, she was beginning to age. Her hair had turned grey and she had been gripped by an illness which would eventually result in crippling disablement. In the summer of 1938 she defied her doctors and rose from her bed at Polesden Lacey in order to attend Ascot, where, 'to make things easier for her, the King and Queen permitted her to use the royal entrance . . .'

In September 1939, war was declared with Germany. According to Carol Kennedy, Mrs Greville 'rose to the shattering turn of events with indomitable spirit. Very old, lame and nearly blind, confined to a wheelchair but still decked out in the dazzling Greville jewels, she continued to attract the great to her salon . . .'

With the onset of the Blitz, Maggie Greville retreated to a suite at the Dorchester Hotel. She continued to dominate her coterie, receiving a constant flow of guests. Her courage never failed and was conspicuous during the worst of the bombing attacks on London. She also retained that slightly malicious sense of humour which had always been one of her chief characteristics. She chose to live at the very top of the hotel, and took 'delight in inviting nervous friends or those of whose war record she disapproved to come and keep her company during the raids.' As Beverley Nichols recalls: 'They seldom refused. It was easier to brave the Luftwaffe than to incur Maggie's displeasure.'

Like Maud Cunard, Mrs Greville sat out the Blitz 'under the table with the telephone and Shakespeare'. She viewed the war as 'a vulgar inconvenience and tried to make the best of it'. On 30 April 1942 she gave a lunch party in her suite at the Dorchester. Guests included Lord Louis Mountbatten – newly-appointed Chief of Combined Operations – the Duke and Duchess of Kent, the Duchess of Buccleuch and Mr (afterwards Sir) Henry 'Chips' Channon.

By birth an American, but in disposition more English than the English, 'Chips' Channon was an acute observer of the social round. He was quick to notice that Mrs Greville detested being upstaged. When Neville Chamberlain's wife flew to Rome to meet Mussolini in an endeavour to promote Anglo-Italian concord, he wrote in his diary that Mrs Greville remarked: 'Dear woman. How good of her. Still . . . it wouldn't be the first time Rome's been saved by a goose.'

Similarly, when the ancient Alice Keppel – Edward VII's last mistress – was holding every London dinner table in thrall with an account of how she had managed to escape from France, staying one step ahead of the advancing Germans, Mrs Greville was heard to mutter: 'To hear Alice talk, you would think she had swum the Channel with her maid between her teeth.'

On 15 September 1942, at the age of 75, the Honourable Mrs Ronnie Greville died in her suite at the Dorchester. Polesden Lacey was bequeathed to the National Trust. A diamond and emerald necklace, formerly the property of Marie Antoinette, was left to the present Queen Mother. Princess Margaret, of whom Mrs Greville had been especially fond, received a legacy of £20,000.

Her memorial service, at St Mark's, North Audley Street, in the very heart of Mayfair, was attended by seven ambassadors. Also present were Lord Mountbatten, the Lord Chancellor, Osbert and Sachaverell Sitwell and members of the peerage too numerous to catalogue.

The personal contents of her two homes were put up for auction. On 22 March 1943:

> 200 dealers converged on Christie's . . . for a sale of wines, spirits and liqueurs from Polesden Lacey and 16 Charles Street . . . Among the items of sale were 1,000 bottles of claret and six rare bottles of Grande Champagne 1810 brandy. Altogether the sale raised £6,000.

★   ★   ★

Following Mrs Greville's death, 16 Charles Street stood empty for three years. But on 28 September 1945 the national newspapers carried reports that it had been acquired by the Guards' Club.

The Guards' Club has a long and distinguished history. Strictly speaking, it was the first authentic 'Gentleman's Club' to be formed – in 1810, the year the best of Mrs Greville's brandy was being laid down.

It was also the first London Club to be owned exclusively by its members. The others – such as Brooks's, White's and Boodle's – were proprietary. Known as 'subscription houses', they were essentially little more than gaming dens run by businessmen for their own profit. As such, they could be – and frequently were – bought and sold over the heads of the members.

The Guards' Club owes its genesis to the Peninsular War – when London was thronged with officers either awaiting a posting or home on leave. Their only recourse was the coffee-house, the chop-house or one or other of the more fashionable gaming dens. According to Graves, writing in *Leather Armchairs*:

> The Prince Regent and the Duke of Wellington both felt concerned that Guards officers had nowhere inexpensive and respectable to spend their leaves. Finally . . . it was decided to create a rendezvous in the St James's Coffee House at the bottom of St James's Street, opposite Lock's the Hatter. According to Captain Gronow . . . it was a miserable little place, with the floor sanded as if it were a tap room.
>
> After the Battle of Waterloo, members of the club set up their first real home at 49 St James's Street, opposite White's. The club remained there for a number of years before moving to No. 70 Pall Mall. In those days, military protocol was stiffly maintained. An ensign would not dare stand in front of the fireplace. He had to rise when a senior officer came in and evening dress was compulsory at dinner.

Each year, the club closed for a period to allow it to be thoroughly cleaned and refurbished. During this time the members found a temporary billet with the Oxford and Cambridge Club, next door at No. 71. Unlike the Guards', the Oxford and Cambridge was an amiable, relaxed sort of establishment. It even served free barley water to members' horses. It was also sumptuously appointed.

On the first morning of one of these temporary billetings, a young Guards' officer strolled into the Oxford and Cambridge and threw himself into the most comfortable chair. After casting his eye around approvingly, he remarked to his neighbour – whose features were concealed behind a newspaper: 'By Jove, you chaps of the middle class do yourselves well.' The newspaper was lowered and the Guards officer found himself staring at the stony features of the Duke of Wellington.

★ ★ ★

At the outbreak of the First World War in 1914 the army acquired a host of new officers and the Guards' Club a host of new members. With the increased revenue generated by their subscriptions, it was able to acquire magnificent premises in Brook Street. However, by 1945 membership had again increased and the move was made to 16 Charles Street, which thus became the club's fifth home in 135 years. It had no sooner taken up residence than dry rot was discovered.

The hall porter at this date was Fred Lloyd. In the course of researching this report, I sought him out. Now past eighty years of age, he joined the club in 1921 as a boy of fourteen, earning ten shillings (fifty pence) a week. He paid no income tax – 'it didn't apply to working people like us' – but recalls that the Committee 'stopped threepence (1p.) a week from our wages for breakages, whether we broke anything or not. I suppose they thought if you didn't break a dish this week you'd probably break two the next.'

Lloyd worked with 'little Frankie Tyrell, now the hall porter at Bucks' Club. Their hours were long, from eight in the morning until seven at night. Their duties included pigeon-holing the mail of members staying at the club, and forwarding that of those who were not. They had also to take scrupulous care over signing members in and out – even though they might only have stepped into the street for a smoke and a breath of fresh air – in order that enquirers might know where to find them.

The staff numbered about a hundred, one for every twenty members. Tipping was forbidden but members were encouraged to subscribe to two annual staff 'lists', for Christmas and the summer holidays, when the staff were officially on leave. One says 'officially' because the Christmas fortnight was spent spring-cleaning. Those members of staff not required for this, or considered too ancient to cope with this more strenuous work, were seconded to other clubs on a reciprocal basis, usually for the more menial and time-consuming tasks.

The cellars, being those of a private house, were large. Nonetheless, they were not really adequate for the laying down of wine on the scale required by a club. This apart, No. 16 adapted itself to its new role rather well. The barman perfected a breath-taking martini; and the chef established a reputation for excellent *lobster bisque* and *tournedos Rossini*. Lunch, at seven

The smoking-room of the club

shillings and sixpence (37p.), was equivalent to three-quarters of Fred Lloyd's starting wage.

On entering the building, members first encountered the morning-room, which was situated on the right of the hallway and possessed a number of red leather armchairs. The card room, also on the ground floor, accommodated several very indifferent portraits, including one of Lord Alexander of Tunis. It is said that when Lord Alexander saw this for the first time he failed to recognize himself and said: 'I shouldn't think anyone stops to look at that old bastard.'

The third salon on the ground floor was the members' bar. The fourth was the coffee room which boasted a magnificent table, seating eight. Known as 'the Cads' Table', it was reserved for the use of members only. A passageway led through to the dining-room at the rear of the property. The last of the ground-floor rooms was the barber's shop.

The walls of the stairs leading to the basement lavatories were lined with cartoons. One of these, by Giles, depicted a Guards officer 'whacking with his tightly rolled umbrella the backside of a fat American female tourist who is embarrassing a sentry outside Buckingham Palace.'

Upstairs was a cocktail bar where male and female members could meet. There was also a smoking room; a small washroom, with hand-basins; toilets;

a private dining-room; and the ladies' drawing-room still ornamented with the eighteen carat gold-leaf and scrollwork placed there by Mewes & Davis at the behest of Maggie Greville.

The rest of the house was given over to offices for senior club staff; and some thirty bedrooms for country members.

Because the house immediately adjacent to the club had been destroyed during the Blitz, members were able to use the site as a car park. Plans to redevelop this, providing a swimming pool and an additional garden, came

The ladies' drawing-room of the Guards' Club

to nothing as a result of lengthy territorial disputes.

Although there was a certain amount of horseplay on stag nights, members of the club (being military men and used to discipline) seldom misbehaved at other times. As Fred Lloyd explained, 'We clamped down on sky-larking through the day.'

Non-members, however, were a different matter and a constant source of irritation. Fortunately, the hall porters had their own diplomatic methods of identifying gate-crashers. Fred Lloyd again:

> You developed a sixth sense about intruders. If they came into the hall and simply looked lost . . . well that was easy enough. The difficult ones were the ones that breezed past you, faces turned the other way, calling out 'Good morning!' as if they'd known you all their lives. Then they'd bolt for the bar.
>
> It didn't usually work. We might have had two thousand members, but we knew most of 'em by sight. If we didn't, we used to follow 'em. Of course, you couldn't challenge 'em outright. The Secretary wouldn't have stood for it. They might be gate-crashers, but most of 'em were gentlemen.
>
> So we used to say: 'Excuse me sir, are you lorst?' Most of 'em took the lifeline – that they'd got lost, was in the wrong club. If they tried to brazen it out, we'd say: 'I don't recall your name, sir. Could you just tell it me again? We might be holding some mail for you.' Then we'd nip back to the porters' desk and check it against the Members' Register. But mostly it didn't come to that. They knew when we was on to them.'

The club possessed a number of curiosities including a 'scrap-book screen' which showed 'Edwardian and Victorian characters – judges, field-marshals, jockeys, priests, old gentlemen helping ladies to undo their corsets, and other entertaining scenes'. There were several battle-stained Scots Guards Colours hanging above the staircase; and an Elizabethan slipper which had been unearthed in an attic of the club's former premises in Brook Street.

There are numerous amusing stories attaching to the club. Some of them may be true. There is the case of Brigadier Mills-Roberts, who booked into Room 10. Returning late and 'happy', he inadvertently got into bed with Colonel Edgar Brassey in Room 11; neither bothered to salute.

Another story concerns a night porter who was seriously frightened, at three o'clock in the morning, when in the half-light he observed a white shape floating down the staircase. It proved to be nothing more terrifying than Colonel Charles Wild who, finding himself unable to sleep, had come to look for a book in the library.

A third anecdote is of Captain Bruce Wentworth, who called for a taxi to take him to Victoria Station. Rather absentmindedly, he made the mistake of placing his luggage in the taxi queueing behind. After he had rattled off in the first, the second one pulled up at the door. When he was unable to locate his 'fare', the club secretary sent him off in pursuit of the first.

Meanwhile, on reaching Victoria, Captain Wentworth realized his mistake and returned to the club – only to be told that the second cab, and his luggage, had gone on the station. 'This happened no less than three times and the situation became wilder and wilder. Finally, both the second taxi-cab driver and Captain Wentworth were told to stay where they were and a rapprochement was effected.'

Members of the Guards' Club have a reputation for bravery which, like Herbert Magniac's, sometimes verged on the suicidal. One such was the unnamed major referred to by Michael Nelson in his book, *Nobs and Snobs*. During the Second World War this gentleman led his men into battle armed only with a shepherd's crook. (Not surprisingly, he was blown to pieces.)

In peacetime, members tended to be no less eccentric. In September 1969 the *Guardian* published an article under the title *Avaunt guards?* in which it asked:

> Where can one go to see a proper English gentleman? The Guards' Club in Charles Street: they're all gentlemen there. Where can one lunch on nice roast lamb and sago pudding before setting off for swimming at the International Sportsman's Club? Where can one chat about the good old days at Caterham? Where can one reminisce about one's japes at Eaton Hall? Where do members still own bowlers? Where are men found still referring to elderly women as 'old bags' and to pretty girls as 'fruits'?
>
> In a way I am delighted that the Guards' Club, which was threatened by a merger with the Cavalry Club (a more boorish and of course a more horsey institution) seems for the moment to have had a reprieve. For there is a special atmosphere, a daft, old-world self-confidence, still obvious at the Guards' Club.
>
> Where else are there such nicknames? Why is Jeremy called Bagot? It is a mystery which no one bothers to explain. Where else are there acres of such sober City suiting, and cavalry twill trousers, and blue blazers for the weekend? Where are there such moustaches, so well kept and military? Where are there such red faces as that man's behind *The Times*? Where are there such high spirits; where else is the club dining-room from time to time the scene of bladish battles with bread rolls?

★ ★ ★

Sadly, the inevitable could not be postponed indefinitely. The club was under-used and this led to financial problems. On 1 January 1976 the Guards' Club vacated 16 Charles Street and moved in with the 'boorish' and 'horsey' Cavalry Club in Piccadilly. Fred Lloyd, the Guards' Club's oldest and most faithful servant, went with them to look after 'his' gentlemen. At the time of writing he is still doing so, 67 years after first joining up. As an article published in *Country Life* in November 1987 attests, his familiar utterances, such as:

> 'I remember your great-grandfather, sir' are an important part of the rich fabric of which this, the world's first and foremost military club, is woven.

According to a newspaper report, everything in Charles Street was sold off. 'Officers with stern faces and long memories sat in the old smoking room . . . as the furniture and fittings went under the auctioneer's hammer.'

The building's contents fetched £38,000 – £20,000 of this being realized in the first ninety minutes of bidding. A chandelier went for £1,200; a mahogany long-case clock, which had formerly graced the hall, fetched £1,000. Members packed the rooms, 'bidding sky-high prices' for everything from chairs to the coffee-making machines in the kitchens.

The sale over, the building was padlocked and left to its memories. A short time later there was a break-in: specialist thieves ripped out and spirited away the beautiful and very valuable marble fireplaces. To date, no arrests have been made. The file at Vine Street police station remains open.

Owing to unforeseen difficulties entailed upon the construction of Rosebery House, on the site adjoining, the redevelopment of 16 Charles Street was long delayed. It was at this stage that I first encountered it, locked and patiently waiting for the next stage in its history to begin.

At the time of writing, reconstruction has started. It is being carried out in a respectful manner, and all the period rooms are expected to be restored to their former splendour.

The refurbishment will provide something in excess of 20,000 square feet of office accommodation. The existing courtyard, at the centre of the development, where Mrs Ronnie Greville once entertained her guests to tea on balmy summer afternoons, will be enclosed by a 'period' conservatory. This, together with a first-floor walkway, will link the old and newer parts of the building.

* * *

If 16 Charles Street is presently filled with rubble – and with workmen who care little if nothing for its past – something of that past yet remains. One man associated with the development dislikes walking around on cold, dark evenings. 'I feel somebody's walking with me, unseen.'

Could it be the shade of Lady Fitzgerald or her daughter, who burned to death so tragically in Charles Street in 1815?

If, as I have heard it suggested, no sight or sound is ever entirely lost, when the pneumatic drills are silenced, and the workmen depart, and the dust settles, do the images of the past reassert themselves? Is the house once again filled with muted laughter and the tinkle of Baccarat crystal as Mrs Ronnie Greville's two permanently inebriated butlers – decanters precariously balanced on silver salvers – totter genteelly from one end of the dining-room to the other?

Does the shade of the first Earl Craven still draw pictures of cocoa trees for Harriette Wilson? Are the measured footfalls still occasionally heard here an echo of the Earl's wife, the beautiful 'Covent Garden actress', Louisa Brunton, pacing back and forth as she learns her lines for some long-forgotten private theatrical? Or are they those of Lord Sondes' butler, Edis, doing his nightly rounds to secure the doors and window latches? Is that low murmur the idling engine of some parked car? Or the third Earl Craven railing against the family curse as he draws upon his Craven A?

Is that tap, tap, tap, the sound of some loose wire blowing in the wind; or the bounce of a ghostly ball as the young Sir Douglas Dawson strives – eternally – to repeat the feat of taking nine wickets in three overs in a house match at Eton? Could that curious smell *really* be roast lamb and sago pudding, ordered by some major-general now turned to dust?

No doubt it isn't. But it would be a brave man who dismissed such ideas out of hand. Buildings are more than bricks and mortar or timber and thatch. They are a palimpsest on which every occupant has left an imprint.

To that degree the past and those who occupied it still exist . . . are still with us.

Appendix

County Record Offices in England

AVON

Bath City Record Office
Guildhall, Bath BA1 5AW
Tel: 0225 61111 Ext. 201
Open: M–Th 9–1, 2–5; F 9–1, 2–4.30

Bristol Record Office
The Council House, College Green, Bristol
BS1 5TR
Tel: 0272 266031 Ext. 442
Open: M–Th 9.30–4.45; F 9.30–4.15;
Sat 9–12
Closed last two weeks Jan

BEDFORDSHIRE

Bedfordshire Record Office
County Hall, Bedford MK42 9AP
Tel: 0234 228833 Ext. 2833
Open: M–F 9.15–1, 2–5

BERKSHIRE

Berkshire Record Office
Shire Hall, Shinfield Park, Reading
RG2 9XD
Tel: 0734 875444 Ext. 3182
Open: M 2–5; T–W 9–5; Th 9–9; F 9–4.30
Closed two weeks Oct/Nov

BUCKINGHAMSHIRE

Buckinghamshire Record Office
County Hall, Aylesbury HP20 1UA
Tel: 0296 395000 Ext. 587
Open: T–Th 9–5.15; F 9–4.45
Closed second week Feb

CAMBRIDGESHIRE

Cambridgeshire Record Office
Shire Hall, Cambridge CB3 0AP
Tel: 0223 317281
Open: M–Th 9–12.45, 1.45–5.15;
F 9–12.45, 1.45–4.15

Cambridgeshire Record Office
Grammar School Walk, Huntingdon
PE18 6LF
Tel: 0480 425842
Open: M–Th 9–12.45, 1.45–5.15;
F 9–12.45, 1.45–4.15
Also open the second Saturday of each month
from 9–12

CHESHIRE

Cheshire Record Office
Duke Street, Chester CH1 1RL
Tel: 0244 602574
Open: M–F 9.45–4.30

Chester City Record Office
Town Hall, Chester CH1 2HJ
Tel: 0244 40144 Ext. 2108
Open: M–F 9–1, 2–5

CLEVELAND

Cleveland County Archives Department
Exchange House, 6 Marton Road,
Middlesbrough TS1 1DB
Tel: 0642 248321
Open: M–Th 9–1. 2–4.30; F 9–1. 2–4

CORNWALL

Cornwall Record Office
County Hall, Truro TR1 3AY
Tel: 0872 73698 Ext. 3127
Open: T–Th 9.30–1, 2–5; F 9.30–1, 2–4.30;
Sat 9–12
Closed first two weeks Dec

CUMBRIA

Cumbria Record Office (Carlisle)
The Castle, Carlisle CA3 8UR
Tel: 0228 23456 Ext. 2416
Open: M–F 9–5

Cumbria Record Office (Kendal)
County Offices, Kendal LA9 4RQ
Tel: 0539 21000 Ext. 329
Open: M–F 9–5

Cumbria Record Office (Barrow)
140 Duke Street, Barrow-in-Furness
LA14 1XW
Tel: 0229 31269
Open: M–F 9–5

DERBYSHIRE

Derbyshire Record Office
County Offices, Matlock DE4 3AG
Tel: 0629 3411 Ext. 7347
Open: M–F 9.30–1, 2–4.45

DEVON

Devon Record Office
Castle Street, Exeter EX4 3PU
Tel: 0392 273509
Open: M–Th 9.30–5; F 9.30–4.30
Also first and third Saturday of each month
9.30–12

West Devon Record Office
Unit 3, Clare Place, Coxside, Plymouth
PL4 0JW
Tel: 0752 264685
Open: M–Th 9.30–5 (to 7 on first Wednesday
of each month); F 9.30–4.30

DORSET

Dorset Record Office
County Hall, Dorchester DT1 1XJ
Tel: 0305 204411
Open: M–F 9–1, 2–5

DURHAM

Durham County Record Office
County Hall, Durham DH1 5UL
Tel: 0385 64411 Ext. 2474
Open: M T Th 8.45–4.45; W 8.45–8.30;
F 8.45–4.15

ESSEX

Essex Record Office
County Hall, Chelmsford CM1 1LX
Tel: 0245 267222 Ext. 2104
Open: M 10–8.45; T–Th 9.15–5.15;
F 9.15–4.15

Essex Record Office (Colchester & North
East Branch)
Stanwell House, Stanwell Street, Colchester
CO2 7DL
Tel: 0206 572099
Open: M–Th 9.15–5.15; F 9.15–4.15

Essex Record Office (Southend Branch)
Central Library, Victoria Avenue,
Southend-on-Sea SS2 6EX
Tel: 0702 612621
Open: M–Th 9.15–5; F9.15–4.15

GLOUCESTERSHIRE

Gloucestershire Record Office
Clarence Row, off Alvin Street, Gloucester
GL1 3DW
Tel: 0452 425295
Open: M T W F 9–1, 2–5; Th 9–1, 2–8

HAMPSHIRE

Hampshire Record Office
20 Southgate Street, Winchester SO23 9EF
Tel: 0962 63153
Open: M–Th 9–4.45; F 9–4.15; Sat 9.30–12
(Apr–Sep, second and fourth Saturday only)
Closed last full week before Christmas

Portsmouth City Records Office
3 Museum Road, Portsmouth PO1 2LE
Tel: 0705 829765
Open: M–W 9.30–12.30, 2–5; Th 9.30–
12.30, 2–7; F 9.30–12.30, 2–4

Southampton City Record Office
Civic Centre, Southampton SO9 4XR
Tel: 0703 832251 Ext. 2251
Open: M–F 9–1, 1.30–5 (plus two evenings a
month until 9)

HEREFORD AND WORCESTER

Hereford and Worcester Record Office
County Hall, Spetchley Road, Worcester
WR5 2NP
Tel: 0905 353366 Ext. 3615
Open: M 10–4.45; T–Th 9.15–4.45; F
9.15–4

Hereford Record Office
The Old Barracks, Harold Street, Hereford
HR1 2QX
Tel: 0432 265441
Open: M 10–1, 2–4.45; T–Th 9.15–1, 2–
4.45; F 9.15–1, 2–4

Worcester (St Helen's) Record Office
Fish Street, Worcester WR1 2HW
Tel: 0905 353366 Ext. 3616
Open: M 10–4.45; T–Th 9.15–4.45; F
9.15–4

HERTFORDSHIRE

Hertfordshire Record Office
County Hall, Hertford SG13 8DE
Tel: 0992 555105
Open: M–Th 9.15–5.15; F 9.15–4.30

HUMBERSIDE

Humberside County Record Office
County Hall, Beverley HU17 9BA
Tel: 0482 867131 Ext. 3394
Open: M W Th 9.15–4.45; T 9.15–8;
F 9.15–4
Closed last complete week in Jan

South Humberside Area Record Office
Town Hall Square, Grimsby DN31 1HX
Tel: 0472 353481
Open: M–Th 9.30–12, 1–5; F 9.30–12,
1–4.15

Kingston upon Hull City Record Office
79 Lowgate, Hull HU1 2AA
Tel: 0482 222015
Open: M–Th 8.30–5; F 8.30–4.30

KENT

Kent Archives Office
County Hall, Maidstone ME14 1XQ
Tel: 0622 671411 Ext. 3363
Open: T–F 9–4.30

Kent Archives Office (South East Kent Area)
Central Library, Grace Hill, Folkestone
CT20 1HD
Tel: 0303 57583
Open: M Th 9–6; T F 9–7; W 9–1; Sat 9–5

Kent Archives Office (North East Kent Area)
Ramsgate Library, Guildford Lawn, Ramsgate CT11 9AI
Tel: 0843 593532 Ext. 3
Open: M–W F 9.30–5.30; Th 9.30–5

LANCASHIRE

Lancashire Record Office
Bow Lane, Preston PR1 8ND
Tel: 0772 54868 Ext. 3039
Open: T 10–8.30; W–F 10–5

LEICESTER (including Rutland)

Leicestershire Record Office
57 New Walk, Leicester LE1 7JB
Tel: 0533 544566
Open: M–Th 9.15–5; F 9.15–4.45; Sat 9.15–12.15

LINCOLNSHIRE

Lincolnshire Archives Office
The Castle, Lincoln LN1 3AB
Tel: 0522 25158
Open: M–F 9.15–4.45

GREATER LONDON
(Local History Libraries)

Greater London Record Office
40 Northampton Road, London EC1R 0HB
Tel: 01 633 6851
Open: T–F 10–4.45

Guildhall Library
Aldermanbury, London EC2P 2EJ
Tel: 01 606 3030 Ext. 1863
Open: M–S 9.30–4.45

Barnet Local History Library
Ravensfield House, The Burroughs, London NW4 4BE
Tel: 01 202 5625 Ext. 55
Open: M Th F 9.15–12.15; T W 9.15–5; Sat 9–4

Bexley Local Studies Section
Hall Place, Bourne Road, Bexley DA5 1PQ
Tel: 0322 526574 Ext. 217
Open: M–S 9–5

Brent Leisure Services
Grange Museum of Local History, Neasden Lane, London NW10 1QB
Tel: 01 908 7432
Open: M T Th F 12–5; W 12–8; Sat 10–5

Bromley Archives Section
Central Library, High Street, Bromley BR1 1EX
Tel: 01 460 9955 Ext. 261
Open: T Th 9.30–8; W F 9.30–6; Sat 9.30–5

Camden Local History Library
32–38 Theobalds Road, London WC1X 8PA
Tel: 01 405 2706 Ext. 337
Open: M T 9–8; F 9–6; Sat 9–5

Camden Local History Library
Swiss Cottage Library, 88 Avenue Road, London NW3 3HA
Tel: 01 586 5989 Ext. 234
Open: M T Th 9.30–8; F 9.30–6; Sat 9.30–5

Greenwich Local History Library
Woodlands, 90 Mycenae Road, Blackheath, London SE3 7SE
Tel: 01 858 4631
Open: M T Th 9–8; Sat 9–5

Hackney Archives Department
Rose Lipman Library, De Beauvoir Road, London N1 5SQ
Tel: 01 241 2886
Open: M 2–8; T Th F 9.30–5; Sat 9.30–1, 2–5

Hammersmith and Fulham Archives
Shepherd's Bush Library, 7 Uxbridge Road, London W12 8LJ
Tel: 01 743 0910 Ext. 3850
Open: M T Th F 9.30–5

Haringey Libraries
Bruce Castle Museum, Lordship Lane, London N17 8NU
Tel: 01 808 8722
Open: M–S 1–4.45

Kensington & Chelsea Libraries
Central Library, Phillimore Walk, London W8 7RX
Tel: 012 937 2542 Ext. 3038
Open: M T Th F 10–8; W 10–1; Sat 10–5

Lambeth Archives Department
Minet Library, 52 Knatchbull Road, London SE5 9QY
Tel: 01 733 3279
*Open: Varies almost week by week owing to 'Government cut-backs'.
Check by phone before visiting.
It may be necessary to make an appointment*

Lewisham Local History Centre
The Manor House, Old Road, London SE13 5SY
Tel: 01 852 5050
Open: M F Sat 9.30–5; T Th 9.30–8

Redbridge Central Library
Local History Room, Clements Road, Ilford EG1 1EA
Tel: 01 478 7145
Open: T–F 9.30–8; Sat 9.30–4

Southwark Local Studies Library
211 Borough High Street, London SE1 1JA
Tel: 01 403 3507
*Open: M Th 9.30–12.30, 1.30–8; T F
9.30–12.30, 1.30–5; Sat 9.30–1*

Tower Hamlets Local History Library
277 Bancroft Road, London E1 4DQ
Tel: 01 980 4366 Ext 47
Open: M T Th F 9–8; Sat 9–5

Waltham Forest Archives
Vestry House Museum, Vestry Road,
London E17 9NH
Tel: 01 509 1917 Ext. 4391
*Open: T–F 10.30–1, 2–5.30; Sat 10.30–1,
2–5*

Westminster City Archives
Victoria Library, Buckingham Palace Road,
London SW1W 9UD
Tel: 01 798 2180
Open: M–F 9.30–7; Sat 9.30–1, 2–5

Local History Library
Marylebone Library, Marylebone Road,
London NW1 5PS
Tel: 01 798 1030
Open: M–F 9.30–7; Sat 9.30–1, 2–5

GREATER MANCHESTER

Greater Manchester County Record Office
56 Marshall Street, New Cross, Manchester
M4 5FU
Tel: 061 247 3383
*Open: M F 9–5; T–Th 9–6. Also open on the
second and fourth Sat of each month*

Bolton Archive Service
Central Library, Civic Centre, Le Mans
Crescent, Bolton BL1 1SE
Tel: 0204 22311 Ext. 2179
*Open: M F 9.30–12, 1–4.30; T 9.30–12.30;
Th 1–7*

Bury Archive Service
112 The Rock, Bury BL9 0PD
Tel: 061 764 8625
Open: W 1–7.30 and by appointment

Manchester Archives Department
St Peter's Square, Manchester M2 5PD
Tel: 061 236 9422 Ext. 269
Open: M 9–12, 1–9; T–F 9–12, 1–5

Rochdale Local Studies Department
Area Central Library, Esplanade, Rochdale
OL16 1AQ
Tel: 0706 47474 Ext. 423
*Open: M T Th 9.30–7.30; W 9.30–5; F
9.30–5.30; Sat 9.30–4*

Salford Archives Centre
658–662 Liverpool Road, Irlam, Manchester
M30 5AD
Tel: 061 775 5643
Open: M–F 9–4.30

Stockport Archive Service
Cental Library, Wellington Road South,
Stockport SK1 3RS
Tel: 061 480 7297
Open: M–F 9–8; Sat 9–12

Tameside Local Studies Library
Stalybridge Library, Trinity Street,
Stalybridge SK15 2BN
Tel: 061 338 2708
Open: M T W F 9–7.30; Sat 9–4

Wigan Record Office
Town Hall, Leigh WN7 2DY
Tel: 0942 672421 Ext. 266
Open: M–F 10–4

MERSEYSIDE

Liverpool Record Office & Local History
Department
City Libraries, William Brown Street,
Liverpool L3 8EW
Tel: 051 207 2147 Ext. 34
Open: M–F 9–9; Sat 9–5

St Helen's Local History & Archive Library
Central Library, Gamble Institute, Victoria
Square, St Helen's WA10 1DY
Tel: 0744 24061 Ext. 2952
Open: M–F 9–5; Sat 9–1

Wirral Archives Services
Birkenhead Reference Library, Borough
Road, Birkenhead L41 2XB
Tel: 051 652 6106 Ext. 34
Open: M T Th F 10–8; Sat 10–1, 2–5

WEST MIDLANDS

Birmingham Central Libraries
Archives Department, Chamberlain Square,
Birmingham B3 3HQ
Tel: 021 235 4217
Open: M–F 9–6; Sat 9–5

Coventry City Record Office
Mandela House, Bayley Lane, Coventry
CV1 5RG
Tel: 0203 25555 Ext. 2768
Open: M–Th 8.45–4.45; F 8.45–4.15

Dudley Archives & Local HIstory
Department
Dudley Library, St James Road, Dudley DT9
9EL
Tel: 0384 55433 Ext. 5514
*Open: M W F 9–1,2–5; T Th 2–7. Also the
first and third Sat in each month 9.30–12.30*

Walsall Archives Service
Local History Centre, Essex Street, Walsall
WS2 7AS
Tel: 0922 37305
*Open: T Th F 9.30–5.30; W 9.30–7; Sat
9.30–1*

Wolverhampton Borough Archives
Central Library, Snow Hill, Wolverhampton
WV1 3AX
Tel: 0902 312025 Ext. 37
Open: M–S 10–1, 2–5

NORFOLK

Norfolk Record Office
Central Library, Norwich NR2 1NJ
Tel: 0603 611277 Ext. 262
Open: M–F 9–5; Sat 9–12

NORTHAMPTONSHIRE

Northamptonshire Record Office
Delapre Abbey, London Road, Northampton
NN4 9AW
Tel: 0604 762129
Open: M–Th 9–4.45; F 9–4.30
Also two Saturdays in each month 9–12.15

NORTHUMBERLAND

Northumberland Record Office
Melton Park, North Gosforth,
Newcastle upon Tyne NE3 5QX
Tel: 091 236 2680
Open: M 9–9; T–Th 9–5; F9–4.30

NOTTINGHAMSHIRE

Nottinghamshire Record Office
County House, High Pavement, Nottingham
NG1 1HR
Tel: 0602 504524
Open: M W Th F 9–4.45; T 9–7.15;
Sat 9–12.15

OXFORDSHIRE

Oxfordshire County Record Office
County Hall, New Road, Oxford, OX1 1ND
Tel: 0865 815203
Open: M–Th 9–1, 2–5; F 9–1, 2–4

SHROPSHIRE

Shropshire Record Office
Shirehall, Abbey Foregate, Shrewsbury
SY2 6ND
Tel: 0743 252851
Open: M T Th 9.30–12.40, 1.20–5;
F 9.30–12.40, 1.20–4
Closed two weeks in late autumn

SOMERSET

Somerset Record Office
Obridge Road, Taunton TA2 7PU
Tel: 0823 337600
Open: M–Th 9–4.50; F 9–4.20; Sat 9.15–
12.15

STAFFORDSHIRE

Staffordshire Record Office
Eastgate Street, Stafford ST16 2LZ

Tel: 0785 3121 Ext. 8380
Open: M–Th 9–1, 1.30–5; F 9–1, 1.30–4.30;
Sat 9.30–1

SUFFOLK

Suffolk Record Office
County Hall, Ipswich IP4 2JS
Tel: 0473 230000 Ext. 4235
Open: M–Th 9–5; F 9–4; Sat 9–1, 2–5

Suffolk Record Office (Bury St Edmunds
Branch)
Raingate Street, Bury St Edmonds
IP33 1RX
Tel: 0284 63141 Ext. 2522
Open: M–Th 9–5; F 9–4; Sat 9–1, 2–5

Suffolk Record Office (Lowestoft Branch)
Central Library, Clapham Road, Lowestoft
NR32 1DR
Tel: 0502 66325 Ext. 274
Open: M–Th 9.15–5; F 9.15–6; Sat 9.15–5

SURREY

Surrey Record Office
County Hall, Penrhyn Road,
Kingston upon Thames KT1 2DN
Tel: 01 541 9065
Open: M T W F 9.30–4.45
Also the second and fourth Saturday of each
month 9.30–12.30

Surrey Record Office
Guildford Muniment Room, Castle Arch,
Guildford GU1 3SX
Tel: 0483 573942
Open: T–Th 9.30–12.30, 1.45–4.45
Also the first and third Saturday of each
month 9.30–12.30

EAST SUSSEX

East Sussex Record Office
The Maltings, Castle Precincts, Lewes
BN7 1YT
Tel: 0273 475400 Ext. 12
Open: M–Th 8.45–4.45; F 8.45–4.15

WEST SUSSEX

West Sussex Record Office
County Hall, Chichester PO19 1RN
Tel: 0243 777983
Open: M–F 9.15–12.30, 1.30–5

TYNE & WEAR

Tyne & Wear Archives Service
Blandford House, West Blandford Street,
Newcastle upon Tyne NE1 4JA
Tel: 091 232 6789
Open: M W Th F 8.45–5.15; T 8.45–8.30

Local Studies Centre
Howard Street, North Shields NE30 1LY
Tel: 091 258 2811 Ext. 17
Open: M W Th F 9–1,2–5; T 9–1,2–7

Gateshead Local Studies Collection
Central Library, Prince Consort Road,
Gateshead NE8 4LN
Tel: 091 447 3478
*Open: M T Th F 9.30–7.30; W 9.30–5;
Sat 9.30–1*

WARWICKSHIRE

Warwick County Record Office
Priory Park, Cape Road, Warwick CV34 4JS
Tel: 0926 493431 Ext. 2508
*Open: M–Th 9–1, 2–5.30; F 9–1, 2–5;
Sat 9–12.30*

ISLE OF WIGHT

Isle of Wight County Record Office
26 Hillside, Newport PO30 2EB
Tel: 0983 524031 Ext. 132
Open: M T Th F 9.30–5; W 9.30–8.30

WILTSHIRE

Wiltshire Record Office
County Hall, Trowbridge BA14 8JG
Tel: 022 14 3641 Ext. 3502
Open: M T Th F 9–5; W 9–8.30

NORTH YORKSHIRE

North Yorkshire County Record Office
County Hall, Northallerton DL7 8AD
Tel: 0609 3123 Ext. 2455
Open: M T Th F 8.50–4.50; W 8.50–8.50

York City Archives Department
Art Gallery Buildings, Exhibition Square,
York YO1 2EW
Tel: 0904 51533
Open: M–F 9.30–12.30, 2–5.30

SOUTH YORKSHIRE

Barnsley Archive Service
Central Library, Shambles Street, Barnsley
S70 2JF
Tel: 0226 283241 Ext. 23
*Open: M–W 9.30–1, 2–6; F 9.30–1, 2–5;
Sat: 9.30–1*

Doncaster Archives Department
King Edward Road, Balby, Doncaster
DN4 0NA
Tel: 0302 859811
Open: M–F 9.30–12.30, 2–5

Rotherham Metropolitan Borough
Brian O'Malley Central Library, Walker
Place, Rotherham S65 1JH
Tel: 0709 382121 Ext. 3583
Open: M T F 10–5; W 1–7; Th 10–7; Sat 9–5

Sheffield Record Office
Central Library, Surrey Street, Sheffield
S1 1XZ
Tel: 0742 734756
*Open: M–F 9.30–5.30. Also to 8.30 on the
second Monday of each month*

WEST YORKSHIRE

West Yorkshire Archives
Headquarters and Wakefield Registry of
Deeds, Newcastle Road, Wakefield
WF1 2DE
Tel: 0924 367111 Ext. 2352
Open: M 9–8; T–Th 9–5; F 9–1

West Yorkshire Archives (Bradford)
15 Canal Road, Bradford BD1 4AT
Tel: 0274 731931
Open: M–F 9.30–1, 2–5

West Yorkshire Archives (Calderdale)
Central Library, Northgate House,
Northgate, Halifax HX1 1UN
Tel: 0422 57257 Ext. 2636
Open: M T Th F 10–5.30; W 10–12

West Yorkshire Archives (Kirklees)
Central Library, Princess Alexandra Walk,
Huddersfield HD1 2SU
Tel: 0484 513808 Ext. 207
Open: M–Th 9–8; F 9–4

West Yorkshire Archives (Leeds)
Chapeltown Road, Sheepscar, Leeds
LS7 3AP
Tel: 0532 628339
Open: M–F 9.30–5

County Record Offices in Wales

CLWYD

Clwyd Record Office (Hawarden Branch)
The Old Rectory, Hawarden, Deeside
CH5 3NR
Tel: 0244 532364
Open: M–Th 9–4.45; F 9–5.15

Clwyd Record Office (Ruthin Branch)
46 Clwyd Street, Ruthin LL15 1HP
Tel: 08242 3077
Open: M–Th 9–4.45; F 9–4.15

DYFED

Dyfed Archive Service
(Carmarthenshire Area Record Office)
County Hall, Carmarthen SA31 1JP
Tel: 0267 233333 Ext. 4184
*Open: M–Th 9–4.45; F 9–4.15. Also the first
and third Saturday of each month 9.30–12.30*

Dyfed Archive Service
(Cardiganshire Area Record Office)
County Office, Marine Terrace,
Aberystwyth SY23 2DE
Tel: 0970 617581 Ext. 2120
Open: T–Th 9–1, 2–4.45

Dyfed Archive Service
(Pembrokeshire Area Record Office)
The Castle, Haverfordwest SA61 2EF
Tel: 0437 3707
*Open: M–Th 9–4.45; F 9–4.15. Also the first
and third Saturday of each month 9.30–12.30*

SOUTH GLAMORGAN

Glamorgan Archive Service
Glamorgan Record Office, County Hall,
Cathays Park, Cardiff CF1 3NE
Tel: 0222 820282
Open: T–Th 9–5; F 9–4.30
Covers Mid, South and West Glamorgan

WEST GLAMORGAN

West Glamorgan Area Record Office
County Hall, Oystermouth Road, Swansea
SA1 3SN
Tel: 0792 471 589
Open: M–W 9–12.45, 2–4.45

GWENT

Gwent County Record Office
County Hall, Cwmbran NP44 2XH
Tel: 06333 838838
Open: T–Th 9.30–5; F 9.30–4

GWYNEDD

Gwynedd Archives and Museum Services
(Caernarfon Area Record Office)
Victoria Dock, Caernarfon
Tel: 0286 4121 Ext. 2095
*Open: M T Th F 9.30–12.30, 1.30–5;
W 9.30–12.30, 1.30–7*

Gwynedd Archives and Museum Services
(Dolgellau Area Record Office)
Cae Penarlag, Dolgellau LL40 2YB
Tel: 0341 422341 Ext. 261
Open: M T Th F 9–1, 2–5; W 9–1, 2–7

Gwynedd Archives and Museum Services
(Llangefni Area Record Office)
Shire Hall, Llangefni LL7 7TW
Tel: 0248 750262 Ext. 269
Open: M–F 9–1, 2–5

POWYS

Powys Library Headquarters, Archives
Cefnllys Road, Llandrindod Wells LD1 5LD
Tel: 0597 2212
Open: M–Th 9–5; F 9–4

Archival Sources for Scotland

CENTRAL

Central Regional Council Archives
Department
Old High School, Spittal Street, Stirling
FK8 1DG
Tel: 0786 73111 Ext. 466
Open: M–F 9–5

DUMFRIES AND GALLOWAY

Dumfries and Galloway Regional Library
Service
Ewart Public Library, Catherine Street,
Dumfries DG1 1JB
Tel: 0387 53820
Open: M T W F 10–7.30; Th Sat 10–5

Dumfries Archive Centre
33 Burns Street, Dumfries DG1 2PS
Tel: 0387 69254
Open: T–F 2–5

FIFE

St Andrews University Library
North Street, St Andrews KY16 9TR
Tel: 0334 76161 Ext. 514
Open: M–F 9–1, 2–5; Sat 9–12 during term

GRAMPIAN

Grampian Regional Archives
Old Aberdeen House, Dunbar Street,

Aberdeen AB2 1UE
Tel: 0224 481775
Open: M–F 9–5

Moray District Record Office
Tolbooth, High Street, Forres IV36 0AB
Tel: 0309 73617
Open: M–F 9–12.30, 1.30–4.30

Aberdeen City Archives
Town House, Aberdeen AB9 1AQ
Tel: 0224 642121 Ext. 513
Open: M–F 9.30–12.30, 2–4.30

HIGHLAND

Highland Regional Archive
The Library, Farraline Park, Inverness
Tel: 0463 236463
Open: M–F 9.30–5.30

LOTHIAN

National Library of Scotland
Department of Manuscripts, George IV
Bridge, Edinburgh EH1 1EW
Tel: 031 226 4531
Open: M–F 9.30–8.30; Sat 9.30–1

Scottish Record Office
HM General Register House, Princes
Street, Edinburgh EH1 3YY
Tel: 031 556 6585

Open: M–F 9–4.45.
Closed first two weeks in Nov

Scottish Record Office
West Register House, Charlotte Square,
Edinburgh EH2 4DF
Tel: 031 556 6585
Open: M–F 9–4.45.
Closed the third week in Nov
Contains the National Register of Archives
for Scotland

City of Edinburgh District Council Archives
Department of Administration, City
Chambers, High Street, Edinburgh EH1 1YJ
Tel: 031 225 2424 Ext. 5196
Open: M–Th 9.30–12.30, 2–4.30; F 9.30–
12.30, 2–3.45

ORKNEY

Orkney Archives
The Orkney Library, Laing Street, Kirkwall
KW15 1NW
Tel: 0856 3166 Ext. 5
Open: M–F 9–1, 2–5

SHETLAND

Shetland Archives
44 King Harald Street, Lerwick ZE1 0EQ
Tel: 0595 3535 Ext. 269
Open: M–Th 9–1, 2–5; F 9–1, 2–4

STRATHCLYDE

Strathclyde Regional Archives
Mitchell Library, North Street, Glasgow
G3 7DN
Tel: 041 227 2401
Open M–Th 9.30–4.45; F 9.30–4

Argyll & Bute District Archives
Argyll & Bute District Council, Kilmory,
Lochgilphead PA31 8RT
Tel: 0546 2127 Ext. 120
Open: M–Th 9–1, 2–5.15; F 9–1, 2–4

City of Glasgow, Mitchell Library
201 North Street, Glasgow G3 7DN
Tel: 041 221 7030 Ext. 171
Open: M–F 9.30–9; Sat 9.30–5

TAYSIDE

Dundee District Archive and Record Centre
City Chambers, City Square, Dundee
DD1 3BY
Tel: 0382 23141 Ext. 4494
Open: M–F 9–1, 2–5

Perth and Kinross District Archive
Sandeman Library, 16 Kinnoull Street,
Perth PH1 5ET
Tel: 0738 23329
Open: M–F 9.30–1, 2–5

Archival Source for Northern Ireland

Public Record Office of Northern Ireland
66 Balmoral Avenue, Belfast BT9 6NY
Tel: 0232 661621
Open: M–F 9.15–4.45
Closed first two weeks in Dec

Archival Source for the Isle of Man

Manx Museum Library
Kingswood Grove, Douglas
Tel: 0624 75522
Open: M–F 10–5

Supplementary Sources of Information

ENGLAND

Institute of Agricultural History
& Museum of English Rural Life
University of Reading, PO Box 229,
Whiteknights, Reading RG6 2AG
Tel: 0734 875123 Ext. 7677
Open: M T 9.30–1, 2–5; F 30–1, 2–4.30

British Library
Great Russell Street, London WC1B 3DG
Tel: 01 636 1544 Ext. 7508
Open: M F Sat 9–5; T W Th 9–9

Office of Population Censuses and Surveys
St Catherine's House, 10 Kingsway,
London WC2B 6JP
Tel: 01 242 0262 Ext. 2446
Open: M–F 8.30–4.30
Houses registers of births, deaths and
marriages since 1837

Principal Registry of the Family Division
Somerset House, Strand, London
WC2R 1LP
Tel: 01 936 6960
Open: M–F 10–4.30
Holds wills probated in England and Wales
since 1858

House of Lords Records Office
House of Lords, London SW1A 0PW
Tel: 01 219 3074
Open: M–F 9.30–5
Closed last two weeks in Nov

Imperial War Museum (Archives)
Lambeth Road, London SE1 6HZ
Tel: 01 735 8922
Open: M–F 10–5
Closed last two full weeks in Oct

National Army Museum (Archives)
Royal Hospital Road, London SW3 4HT
Tel: 01 730 0717 Ext. 222
Open: T–Sat 10–4.30

National Maritime Museum (Archives)
Greenwich, London SE10 9NF
Tel: 01 858 4422
Open: M–F 10–5; Sat 10–1, 2–5

Public Record Office
Ruskin Avenue, Kew, Richmond TW9 4DU
and at:
Chancery Lane, London WC2A 1LR
Tel: 01 876 3444
Open: M–F 9.30–5

Royal Air Force Museum (Archives)
Aerodrome Road, Hendon,
London NW9 5LL
Tel: 01 205 2266 ext. 210
Open: M–Sun 10–6 (last admissions 5.30)

Science Museum Library
South Kensington, London SW7 5NH
Tel: 01 589 3456 Ext. 527
Open: M–Sat 10–5.30

Corporation of London Records Office
PO Box 270, Guildhall, London EC2P 2EJ
Tel: 01 606 3030 Ext. 1251
Open: M–F 9.30–4.45

British Library of Political and
Economic Science
10 Portugal Street, London WC2A 2HD
Tel: 01 405 7686 Ext. 2968
Open: M–F 10–5.30 (10–5 during vacations)

King's College, London
The Liddell Hart Centre for Military
Archives, Strand, London WC2R 2LS
Tel: 01 836 5454 Ext. 2187
Open: M–F 9.30–5.30 (9.30–4.30 during
vacations)

British Architectural Library
Royal Institute of British Architects,
66 Portland Place, London W1N 4AD
Tel: 01 580 5533 Ext. 4321
Open: M 10–5; T W Th 10–8; F 10–7;
Sat 10–1.30
Closed in Aug

Institution of Civil Engineers
1–7 Great George Street,
London SW1P 3AA
Tel:01 222 7722 Ext. 232
Open: M–F 9.15–5.30

Institution of Electrical Engineers (Archives)
Savoy Place, London WC2R 0BL
Tel: 01 240 1871 Ext. 336
Open: M–F 10–5

Royal Astronomical Society Library
Burlington House, Piccadilly,
London W1V 0NL
Tel: 01 734 4582
Open: M–F 10–5

Royal College of Physicians of London
11 St Andrew's Place, London NW1 4LE
Tel: 01 935 1174
Open: M–F 9.30–5.30

Royal College of Surgeons of England
35–43 Lincoln's Inn Fields, London
WC2A 3PN
Tel: 01 405 3474 Ext. 8
Open: M–F 10–6
Closed in Aug

Royal Institution of Great Britain
21 Albemarle Street, London W1X 4BS
Tel: 01 409 2992 Ext. 4
Open: M–F 10–5.30

Royal Society
6 Carlton House Terrace, London
SW1Y 5AG
Tel: 01 839 5561 Ext. 259
Open: M–F 10–5

Society of Antiquaries of London
Burlington House, Piccadilly,
London W1V 0HS
Tel: 01 734 0193
Open: M–F 10–5

Society of Friends' Library
Friends House, Euston Road,
London NW1 2BJ
Tel: 01 387 3601
Open: T–F 10–5
Closed for the week immediately before the
Spring Bank holiday.
Also closed one week in Aug

Wellcome Institute for the History of
Medicine
183 Euston Road, London NW1 2BP
Tel: 01 387 4477
Open: M–F 9.45–5.15

Dr Williams's Library
14 Gordon Square, London WC1H 0AG
Tel: 01 387 3727
Open: M W F 10–5; T Th 10–6.30
Closed first two weeks in Aug
Holds information on Nonconformist
congregations in Great Britain

John Rylands University Library
of Manchester
Deansgate, Manchester M3 3EH
Tel: 061 834 5343
Open: M–F 10–5.30; Sat 10–1
Methodist archives and Research Centre

British Geological Survey Library
Keyworth, Nottingham NG12 5GG
Tel: 06077 6111 Ext. 3205
Open: M–F 9–4.30

Royal Greenwich Observatory
Herstmonceux Castle, Hailsham BN27 1RP
Tel: 0323 833171 Ext. 3379
Open M–F 9–5.30

Shakespeare Birthplace Trust Records
Office
Henley Street, Stratford-upon-Avon
CV37 6QW
Tel: 0789 204016
Open: M–F 9.30–1, 2–5; Sat 9.30–12.30

National Railway Museum Library
Leeman Road, York YO2 4XJ
Tel: 0904 21261
Open: T–F 10.30–5

The Royal Commission on Historical
Manuscripts
Quality House, Quality Court,
Chancery Lane, London WC2A 1HP
Tel: 01 242 1198
Open: M–F 9.30–5

British Records Association
Master's Court, The Charterhouse,
Charterhouse Square, London EC1M 6AU
Tel: 01 253 0436
(By the time of publication the BRA may
have moved from this address)

Business Archives Council
185 Tower Bridge Road, London SE1 2UF
Tel: 01 407 6110
Open: M–F 9–5

Society of Genealogists
14 Charterhouse Buildings,
London EC1M 7BA
Tel: 01 251 8799
Open: T F Sat 10–6; W Th 10–8
Closed one week in Feb

WALES

National Library of Wales
Aberystwyth SY23 3BU
Tel: 0970 3816
Open: M–F 9.30–6; Sat 9.30–5

SCOTLAND

General Register Office
New Register House, Edinburgh EH1 3YT
Tel: 031 556 3952
Open: M–Th 9.30–4.30; F 9.30–4

National Library of Scotland
George IV Bridge, Edinburgh EH1 1EW
Tel: 031 226 4531
Open: M–F 9.30–8.30; Sat 9.30–1

Scottish Catholic Archives
Columba House, 16 Drummond Place,
Edinburgh EH3 6PL
Tel: 031 556 3661
Open: M–F 9.30–5.30

Royal College of Physicians and Surgeons of
Glasgow
234–242 St Vincent Street, Glasgow G2 5RJ
Tel: 041 221 6072
Open: M–F 9.30–5.30

Business Archives Council of Scotland
Glasgow University Archives,
The University, Glasgow G12 8QQ
Tel: 041 339 8855 Ext. 5515
Open: M–F 9–5

NORTHERN IRELAND

General Register Office
Oxford House, Chichester Street, Belfast
BT1 4HL
Tel: 0232 235211 Ext. 2329
Open: M–F 9.30–3.30

ISLE OF MAN

General Registry
Finch Road, Douglas, Isle of Man
Tel: 0624 75506
Open: M–F 9–1; 2.15–4.30

GUERNSEY

Greffe
Royal Court House, Guernsey
Tel: 0481 25277
Open: M–F 9–1, 2–4

JERSEY

Judicial Greffe
States Building, 10 Hill Street, Royal
Square, St Helier, Jersey
Tel: 0534 75472
Open: M–F 10–1, 2–5

AUTHOR'S NOTE

To the best of my knowledge and belief, the above information is correct. However, circumstances frequently change – institutions may move away or amend their times of opening. Because of this, and because many archivists will only admit readers by appointment it is always advisable to make a preliminary telephone call before setting out on a visit.